'TIS PITY SHE'S A WHORE
John Ford

REVELS STUDENT EDITIONS

Based on the highly respected Revels Plays, which provide a wide range of scholarly critical editions of plays by Shakespeare's contemporaries, the Revels Student Editions offer readable and competitively priced introductions, text and commentary designed to distil the erudition and insights of the Revels Plays, while focusing on matters of clarity and interpretation.

GENERAL EDITOR David Bevington

Dekker/Rowley/Ford *The Witch of Edmonton*
Ford *'Tis Pity She's a Whore*
Jonson *Volpone Bartholomew Fair*
Kyd *The Spanish Tragedy*
Marlowe *The Jew of Malta Tamburlaine the Great*
Marston *The Malcontent*
Middleton/Rowley *The Changeling*
Middleton or Tourneur *The Revenger's Tragedy*
Webster *The Duchess of Malfi The White Devil*

Plays on women: An Anthology
Middleton *A Chaste Maid in Cheapside*
Middleton/Dekker *The Roaring Girl*
Anon. *Arden of Faversham*
Heywood *A Woman Killed with Kindness*

REVELS STUDENT EDITIONS

'TIS PITY SHE'S A WHORE

John Ford

edited by Derek Roper

based on The Revels Plays edition
edited by Derek Roper,
published by Methuen & Co., 1975

MANCHESTER
UNIVERSITY PRESS

Manchester and New York

distributed exclusively in the USA
by Palgrave

Introduction, critical apparatus, etc.
© Derek Roper 1997

Published by Manchester University Press
Oxford Road, Manchester M13 9NR, UK
and Room 400, 175 Fifth Avenue, New York, NY 10010, USA
http://www.manchesteruniversitypress.co.uk

Distributed exclusively in the USA by
Palgrave, 175 Fifth Avenue, New York, NY 10010, USA

Distributed exclusively in Canada by
UBC Press, University of British Columbia, 2029 West Mall,
Vancouver, BC, Canada V6T 1Z2

British Library Cataloguing-in-Publication data
A catalogue record for this book is available from the British Library

Library of Congress Cataloging-in-Publication data
Ford, John, 1586–ca. 1640.
'Tis pity she's a whore / John Ford: edited by Derek Roper.
p. cm.—(Revels student editions)
'Based on the Revels Plays edition edited by Derek Roper.'
ISBN 0-7190-4359-X
I. Tragedies. gsafd. I. Roper, Derek. II. Series.
PR2524.T5 1997
822'.3—DC20 96-34810

ISBN 0 7190 4359 X *paperback*

First published 1997
10 09 08 07 06   10 9 8 7 6 5 4

Preface

Verbally, the text of this edition is that of the fully modernised Revels Plays edition of 1975. The introduction has been completely rewritten and takes quite a different view of the play from that taken twenty years ago. It includes outlines of alternative or supplementary approaches and suggests further reading, not all of it in the field of literary criticism. I am grateful to the friends who have read or heard parts of the introduction in draft and helped in various ways: Nigel Bawcutt, Michael Hattaway, Lisa Hopkins, Sandy Lyle, Philip Roberts and Sue Wiseman. Special thanks are due to the series editor, David Bevington, whose vigilant supervision has saved me from many errors and who has made many useful suggestions for the commentary. The repunctuation of the text, on somewhat different lines from that of the 1975 edition, is largely his work.

Introduction

John Ford was born of an old Devonshire family, the second son of a well-to-do country gentleman, and was baptised on 17 April 1586.[1] At the age of sixteen he was enrolled in one of the Inns of Court, the Middle Temple. At this period the Inns of Court functioned not only as law schools but as town residences for gentlemen, who might stay indefinitely if they paid their bills. Here they learned courtly behaviour, picked up gossip and fashions, made useful contacts, and (if well-connected, or ambitious and lucky) gained a footing at court, where the Inns had a long tradition of presenting entertainments. Literary talent flourished there: among the poets and playwrights who were at the Middle Temple during Ford's time were John Marston, John Davies and Thomas Carew. In 1629 the playwright William Davenant was rooming there with Edward Hyde, the future Earl of Clarendon. Ford was probably of their circle, which also had connections with the family of John Donne.[2]

Ford remained there for many years; indeed, there is no sign that he ever left. In 1638, when he was fifty-two, a commendatory poem still addressed him as '*Master Iohn* FORD, *of the middle Temple*'. His finances are a mystery: as a second son he would not have been allowed to burden the estate, and when his father died in 1610 Ford inherited only £10. An annuity of £20, which he acquired in 1616, would not have gone far towards the expenses of a gentlemanly life in London. Nor would his writings have brought in anything like enough. Ford was never called to the Bar, but may have found other legal employment. One or more of the aristocratic persons to whom some of his plays were dedicated may have helped, and the dedication to '*Tis Pity* mentions 'a particular engagement' (i.e. obligation) to the Earl of Peterborough. Ford contributed commendatory poems to plays by Webster, Shirley, Massinger and others, and received commendatory poems in return. He presumably enjoyed the society of the Middle Temple, and was also on good terms with members of Gray's Inn, including his namesake cousin John Ford. In 1639 he signed the dedication of *The Lady's Trial*, after

1

which nothing certain is heard of him. The date of his death is unknown.

Four years after arriving at the Temple, Ford published a long poem on the death of the Earl of Devonshire, *Fame's Memorial* (1606), and a prose pamphlet, *Honour Triumphant* (1606), upholding four chivalrous propositions that were defended at a ceremonial tilting during the King of Denmark's visit in July that year. Seven years later he published a long poem seemingly intended to call sinners to repentance, *Christ's Bloody Sweat* (1613). There followed two pamphlets of Stoical moralising, *The Golden Mean* (1613) and *A Line of Life* (1620). By this time Ford may already have begun writing for the stage. *The Witch of Edmonton*, written in collaboration with the professional playwrights Thomas Dekker and William Rowley, was put together and produced at the Phoenix in 1621. In 1623 Ford joined with Dekker in a masque-like work, *The Sun's Darling*, and probably with Rowley and Middleton in a tragi-comedy, *The Spanish Gipsy*. By the end of 1624 he had collaborated in at least three other plays, now lost, in one of which Webster had a share. These collaborations must have helped Ford to find his feet as a dramatist and made him known in the theatre world.

The seven surviving plays written independently by Ford were all published between 1629 and 1639. They are a romantic comedy, *The Lover's Melancholy* (1629); three tragedies, *The Broken Heart*, *'Tis Pity*, and *Love's Sacrifice* (all 1633); a history play, *Perkin Warbeck* (1634); and two more comedies, *The Fancies Chaste and Noble* (1638) and *The Lady's Trial* (1639). These publication dates do not tell us when the plays were written; if they were the property of a company, it was in the company's interest to postpone publication for as long as possible, and some of Beeston's plays were in his repertory for many years before they were printed. A performance referred to on the title-page, or in a dedication, need not be the first performance. *The Lover's Melancholy* was licensed for acting on 24 November 1628, and *The Lady's Trial* on 3 May 1638, so they were probably written not long before these dates. The other plays may have been written at any time after Ford had learned his craft.

His early writings show Ford mastering the rhetoric of several styles of thought: romantic and Platonic love, a Calvinistic kind of Protestantism, Stoic beliefs and the cult of honour. It is not easy to say what his own beliefs were. The most important political debate in his lifetime centred on the role of the monarch, but it is much too simple to assume that a man of gentle birth, who dedicated some of his plays to aristocrats, must have been a supporter of 'monarchical absolutism'.[3] His dedications may suggest some sympathy for those noblemen who felt deprived of their rightful influence in government by royal favourites;[4] and some plays show admiration for aristocratic attitudes, particularly in dignified defeat. None of this helps in reading *'Tis Pity*, where the representatives of nobility do not show to advantage. It is the interplay of attitudes, rather than commitment to any one, that is important here; as Rowland Wymer has argued, it was an advantage to Ford as a dramatist that he had more than one voice.[5]

CONTEXT

Though *'Tis Pity* was not published until 1633, it stands apart from Ford's other independent plays in several respects, and may perhaps have been the first that he wrote. The late Elizabethan and early Jacobean drama had made a great impression on him; all his plays contain echoes of and allusions to it, but *'Tis Pity* has the most striking, with obvious debts to Marlowe's *Tamburlaine* and *Dr Faustus*, Shakespeare's *Romeo and Juliet* and *Othello*, and Webster's *Duchess of Malfi*—all first acted between 1587 and 1614. These plays were still being acted in the 1620s and even later, but in his other plays Ford shows less debt to them and develops different modes. It is also the only one of Ford's independent plays not to be set at a court. Though the Cardinal and the banditti belong to Italy, the speech of the citizen characters and details of the setting locate them in the London of Middleton's comedies; indeed the play has been classified as a 'city tragedy'.[6] The wealthy merchants, Florio and Donado, are characterised as affable and manipulative; the nobility, Soranzo, Grimaldi, Richardetto and Hippolita, as proud, vengeful, violent and treacherous.

Ford did not have to fetch his notions of corruption, revenge and elaborate deadly plots from the earlier drama or from Italy. The year before he arrived at the Middle Temple his great-uncle, Lord Chief Justice Popham, had been imprisoned in Essex House, next door to the Temple, by the conspirators in the Essex rising; according to one source, Essex's sister called on the guards to 'throw her down the head of that old fellow'.[7] Then came the accession of James I; the trial of Ralegh, a travesty of justice presided over by Popham, though Ralegh's judicial murder was postponed until 1618; and the Gunpowder Plot. In 1606 the new Earl of Essex was married to

Frances Howard; in 1613 the marriage was annulled so that Frances could be married to James's favourite, the Earl of Somerset; Sir Thomas Overbury, who had opposed the match, was imprisoned in the Tower, where he died; in 1616 Somerset and his countess were convicted of having slowly poisoned him; James himself presided over both the weddings, which were graced by masques from the Inns of Court, and the trial, when many lurid circumstances came to light.[8] Overbury had been at the Middle Temple with Ford, who may have written the lost pamphlet *Sir Thomas Overbury's Ghost*, entered in the Stationer's Register in 1615 as by 'John Fford gent.'; he certainly contributed elegaic verses to the eighth edition of Overbury's poem *The Wife* (1616). Charles I came to the throne in 1625, but James's last and greatest favourite, the Duke of Buckingham, continued to monopolise power and patronage until he was assassinated in 1628.

Incest as well as murder figured among the scandals of high life. According to rumour, a man who had destroyed the offspring of an affair with his sister by throwing the child into the fire had escaped punishment by transferring an estate to the Lord Chief Justice—again, Ford's great-uncle Popham.[9] There is no certain source for the story of *'Tis Pity*, though there are parallels with a story published in 1615 by François de Rosset. There are also parallels between *'Tis Pity* and Middleton's *Women Beware Women*, which has a sub-plot involving incest between uncle and niece and another resembling the Bergetto group, but we cannot be sure which play came first. (For these and other possible sources see the Revels Plays edition, pp. xxvi–xxxvii.) Incestuous love had been treated in several plays, but either presented as wholly wicked (as in Peele's *David and Bethsabe*, Shakespeare's *Pericles*), or found to be not incestuous at all, owing to mistakes about parentage (as in Beaumont and Fletcher's *A King and No King*, licensed 1611, a play Ford probably remembered). Ford was interested in the brother–sister relationship, which is important in *Love's Sacrifice* and *The Broken Heart*.[10] *'Tis Pity* is the first English play to take incestuous lovers as its main protagonists and treat them with some sympathy; critics still argue about how much.

Most of Ford's plays, including the collaborative pieces, were written for a company managed through various metamorphoses by the actor-entrepreneur Christopher Beeston, and known from 1625 onwards as Queen Henrietta's Men. *'Tis Pity*, like *Love's Sacrifice*, *Perkin Warbeck* and the two later comedies, is said on its title-page to have been acted by this company 'at the Phoenix in Drury-Lane'. The Phoenix was one of the so-called 'private theatres', i.e. it was roofed in and much smaller than the open-air theatres of the Globe type; its capacity has been estimated at 500 persons.[11] Designs by Inigo Jones believed to be for the Phoenix show a horseshoe-shaped auditorium with galleries all round, elegant Palladian doorways left and right of the stage, a larger central entrance that could be curtained off and used to begin scenes like II.ii and III.vi, and a gallery stage above. The main stage, a wooden structure not shown in the designs, would have been about 7 m × 4.5 m, and the seating in the pit was gently raked. The narrow windows would not have let in much light, and no direct daylight fell on the stage; probably all performances in the private theatres were given by the light of candles in wall sockets, chandeliers and candelabra. It was an intimate theatre well suited for night sequences like III.vi–ix. The audience would have included courtiers and men from the Inns of Court, and must generally have been better off than the audiences of the open-air theatres, because admission was much more expensive. However, research in the last twenty years suggests that earlier descriptions of an exclusive 'coterie' theatre were exaggerated. The Phoenix was a commercial operation and needed the support of ordinary citizens if it was to survive; and the drama of the private theatres includes a fair amount of criticism, usually oblique, of the king and his court.[12]

Besides the Phoenix Beeston ran a large open-air theatre, the Red Bull, transferring plays and players between the two houses.[13] The Red Bull favoured a broader and noisier style of acting, but there was a good deal of overlap between the repertories, and *The Duchess of Malfi*, in which intimate scenes are important, was first acted at the Red Bull. We have no evidence that any of Ford's plays was performed there; but printers sometimes omitted this less prestigious theatre from their title-pages,[14] and *'Tis Pity* may have been staged at the Red Bull as well as at the Phoenix. (One of two plays that Ford wrote for the King's Men, *The Lover's Melancholy*, was certainly acted at the open-air Globe as well as the private Blackfriars.) A scene like IV.iii would have played well at the Red Bull; and V.vi, which involves seven speaking characters, attendants, a troop of banditti, a banquet and a sword-fight, might have shown to more advantage on its larger stage. In daylight playing, the 'wax lights' and the dark lantern called for in III.vi–vii would have indicated a night scene.

A READING OF THE PLAY

When Giovanni calls the concept of incest 'a customary form, from man to man' (I.i.25), he is reaching towards a truth. Incest is a social construction attached to a relatively unimportant biological fact. To many the very idea is repugnant, yet human beings have no inborn aversion from it. Brothers and sisters are not usually conscious of 'feeling that way' about each other, but that is also true of men and women brought up together but unrelated by blood.[15] By contrast, persons who are closely related may feel strongly attracted sexually if they are brought up apart and ignorant of the blood link. Horror of incest is a product of culture and of particular family structures, and even in a given culture may not be universal: a study of church court records in Tudor and Stuart England found that 'ordinary people' (mostly the rural poor) had no particular horror of it.[16] Where the horror is experienced, it is explained by Freud as resulting from an unconscious mixture of desire and fear: sexual desire (basically for a parent) formed in infancy, together with the dread of being punished for it. In Freud's view this basic conflict explains the origin of the widespread taboo;[17] more certainly, where such conflicts exist they intensify the cultural conditioning. Within the nuclear type of family, incest between a parent and a child is likely to be harmful to the child. Between brother and sister, so long as no coercion is used, it is much less likely to lead to harm, though results differ widely. Such relationships are often brief and seem to have no significant consequences; in other cases they can lead either to revulsion, or to intense pleasure and a long-lasting happy relationship.[18]

Incest has been prohibited in almost all known societies[19] from prehistoric times until quite lately, though 'the relativity of the laws governing incest is every bit as striking as their alleged universality'.[20] The Jewish prohibitions are extensive and are set out in Leviticus xviii.6–18, whence they passed into Christian teaching. In England the main sanction has been a religious one, and in Ford's day incest could only be dealt with by the church courts; but secular arguments were used to support the religious ban. The ill effects produced by generations of close breeding were known and exaggerated. Incest was said to be so unnatural that even the nobler animals avoided it; it was believed that such unions would be sterile, or produce 'monsters', an idea latent in Hippolita's curse (IV.i.97–100). But the sceptical temper of the seventeenth century had begun to question whether 'nature' did always reinforce religion, and in 1625 the jurist Grotius had included incest among practices which, though forbidden by God, were not necessarily contrary to natural law.[21] A traditional argument against incest was that where sexual passion was reinforced by close sympathy arising from kinship, it would be so strong as to be ungovernable.[22] When he woos Annabella, Giovanni inverts both these arguments: 'wise Nature' meant us for each other, and our kinship makes us better lovers (I.ii.235–41). And later in the play the Friar seems to surrender the case from nature and rest the prohibition wholly on religion, since 'nature is in heaven's positions blind' (II.v.34).

But the strongest secular argument was that in the prevailing discourse incest was seen as a challenge to the moral, social, and even political order. The rise of more authoritarian styles of government in Renaissance England brought with it an increased emphasis on the ideal of the family as both unit and image of the national hierarchy, held together by bonds of love and discipline and controlled by patriarchal authority. But sexual love, which should bind husband and wife together, could, if misplaced, be a strong force to disrupt the family; and incest was the most disruptive form of it, destroying 'reverence' by throwing all relationships into confusion. As the Bishop of Bath and Wells pointed out in 1629,

> *Fornication* violateth the good order that should be betweene single persons, through unruly Lusts; *Adulterie* addeth thereunto a confusion of Families, and taketh away the distinction of Heires, and Inheritance; but *Incest* moreover abolisheth the reverence which is ingraved by nature, to forbid that persons whom nature hath made so neere should one uncover the others shame.[23]

It is because his sexual preference constitutes such a challenge to every aspect of authority that Giovanni has to borrow the rebellious eloquence of Tamburlaine and Faustus to defend it.

Audiences at the Phoenix may have thrilled in response to such a rebellion, but they are unlikely to have endorsed it; and the same is true of Ford himself. To a large extent Ford, like other dramatists, was working not only within the beliefs and assumptions of his society but within the kinds of discourse, the ways of presenting and judging men and women, that were current. Nevertheless, an imaginative writer is not wholly trapped within these traditions but can modify them, which is one reason why we value such writers. By making sibling lovers the central figures in a tragedy—a new departure—Ford showed himself willing to give them some sympathy, since this was necessary for the tragic effect; and his presentation of their society is more like a satire upon the established order than a defence of it. The overt narrative of *'Tis Pity* tells of the downfall of two guilty lovers, but inscribed within this narrative is another telling of the destruction of love and trust in a world where such things are rare. Moreover, each narrative criticises itself: the lovers fail, in different ways, as lovers, and Parma fails by the standards it proclaims. The catastrophe may be inevitable, but the voices that greet it as a triumph of divine justice are heard with total scepticism. Such a play should not be read as a closed text imposing a single view, but as an open or 'interrogative' one, inviting the audience or reader to find their bearings among competing discourses.

Ford has not shown or related the process by which Giovanni and Annabella fall in love, but the social and family circumstances are clear. They are the only children of a wealthy bourgeois family in Parma (I.iii.4–9, II.ii.49); in their social class girls and boys would not be brought up in the physical intimacy of a poorer family. But emotional relations between brother and sister could be very close indeed at this period; and if the boy was kept at home until he was sent to university, there was time for these relationships to mature and deepen.[24] For Giovanni and Annabella this relationship apparently turns to love—as in the possible source story by de Rosset— after the brother's return from college, when he and his sister, now physically mature, rediscover each other.

The first scene is a swift and shocking piece of exposition. On the stage any figure of youth, energy and passion, pleading only to be allowed to love, must win some sympathy when opposed to one of age, authority and restraint, especially (for a Protestant audience) when the authority figure is clad as a friar. But sympathy is checked, not only by our realisation of what Giovanni demands, but by the way the text defines him. Like Marlowe's Faustus he is a brilliant scholar, yet as with Faustus his speech signals this as an unsound brilliance, corrupted by passion and pride. (His habits of solitude and hard study, mentioned by Florio at I.iii.5–6 and II.vi.126–8, would suggest to contemporaries a man of 'melancholy humour', vulnerable to excessive and morbid passions.) The arguments by which he justifies incest in this scene are the stage equivalent of the false reasoning by which a clever man might deceive himself, like Faustus's misreading of the scriptures, and like his own pseudo-syllogisms in II.v. His dismissal of the blood relationship as 'a customary form' is immediately offset by the concreteness of 'one womb'; and the violence of 'Curse to my joys!' makes it obvious that frustration rather than logic is speaking (I.i.25–9). Likewise the rhythmic drive of his language passes over into Tamburlaine-like bombast (I.i.64–5). In this exchange the Friar proves the more impressive figure of the two: his role resembles that of Faustus's Good Angel, and his speech, by its grave concern and compassionate tone, recalls that of the Old Man in the same play.

The second scene begins with a parade of Annabella's suitors: Grimaldi the noble coward, Soranzo the adulterer and Bergetto the idiot. Destined for one of these men, and protected by a 'guardian' whose coarse cynical speech ironises her title, Annabella is so placed as to be grateful for her brother's love; and the pattern of the scene suggests a folk-tale or wooing game, where Giovanni's appearance as the last suitor in the series makes him a likely winner. This wooing is not easy: brother-and-sister intimacy (177–9) gets nowhere and is abandoned in impatience; praise in the tradition of the Elizabethan sonneteers (193–204) is taken as a joke; the offer of his dagger is a last exasperated attempt to convince Annabella of the life-and-death meaning of what he says. At first she responds with surprise and fear: 'If this be true, 'twere fitter I were dead' (221). Giovanni over-whelms her with convincing passion, with arguments that she can-not combat as the Friar can, and finally with a desperate lie, telling her that his love is sanctioned by 'the holy Church' (242–3).[25] After the anguished climax of his speech, Annabella's unexpected surren-der, not only to Giovanni but to a passion of which she had not before allowed herself to be fully conscious (245–52), comes as a relief; and with this response she flowers into expressive speech for the first time. The whole scene, culminating in the ritual exchange of vows, is well imagined and beautifully written, and raises sympa-thy for the lovers to its highest point. Giovanni's assertion that their love is the work of 'wise Nature' (237) seems borne out by the experience we share when the two walk off hand in hand, to do something as happy and natural as 'to kiss and sleep'. We do not, though, forget Giovanni's lie or the unscrupulousness of his passion.

In the following scene we see more of their father, Florio, usually described by critics as 'kindly'; and indeed his speech to them is affectionate, with none of the tyrannical railing of Old Capulet. His professed intentions for Annabella too are liberal for the age: 'I would not have her marry wealth, but love', he tells Bergetto's uncle Donado (I.iii.1–13). An arranged marriage with an idiot, if advantageous to the family, would not have been out of the question at this period: Richardetto 'counsels' his niece Philotis to prepare to marry Bergetto without Donado's knowledge (III.v.27–34), obviously because Bergetto will be heir to his uncle's fortune (I.iii.69–76).[26] That kind of match, between Richardetto's nobility and Donado's wealth from trade, was becoming more common in seventeenth-century England; and that is what Florio has in mind for Annabella. He has (we hear later) considered Grimaldi, whose uncle is a duke, but decided against him (I.ii.78, III.ix.57–9). The nobleman he prefers is Soranzo, though Soranzo's adulterous affair with Hippolita is known throughout Parma (IV.i.42–3). Florio has already promised Annabella to Soranzo and told him that he has her heart (I.ii.54–5); and Soranzo is conscious of the advantages of the match (III.ii.32–3). Florio's pretence that Annabella has a free choice can only be a way of keeping things smooth with Donado by letting her give Bergetto his refusal herself. It is ironical that when we hear of her freedom to choose for love we know both that she is not to be given it, and that she has already taken it, and chosen her brother. By the end of the first act their passion and their society have been set on course for collision; also, a lie has been exposed within each.

When Giovanni and Annabella reappear in II.i, the positive power of unorthodox love comes over strongly in a scene of happy intimacy and affectionate teasing. Her words do at least as much as his to establish this power, and less to undermine it. They reject the traditional notion (seen for example in Spenser's *Epithalamion*, 223–41) that a modest woman should blush at the thought of sexual pleasure even in wedlock; for her, love has banished this shame:

> . . . O, how these stol'n contents
> Would print a modest crimson on my cheeks,
> Had any but my heart's delight prevailed!   (II.i.6–8)

But it soon appears that though incest has made Giovanni a rebel against patriarchal order, he is himself the patriarch of their new secret world. He is Annabella's 'king' (19), as in the last scene he will look back on their relationship as a monarchy (V.vi.45); he commands her to be faithful as a legitimate husband might do. He does in fact regard their mutual vows as a form of marriage, one that will prove as cruel in the end as anything the other suitors could have offered. (At II.vi.37–43 we find that he has confirmed it by asking for the gift of a particularly significant ring.) Annabella accepts this relationship, closing their dialogue with a quiet tender couplet.

Putana's coarse comment reduces love to a bodily urge in a way that at first seems inappropriate: 'I say still, if a young wench feel the fit upon her, let her take anybody, father or brother, all is one' (II.i.48–50). Yet her words act as a reductive parody of what fully liberated sexual love, guided only by 'wise Nature', might mean. They have more power because they are in keeping with Giovanni's new foregrounding of the physical, in his remarks about maidenhead as a 'pretty toy' which, lost, becomes 'nothing', and his metaphor for lovemaking (II.i.9–14). Although Giovanni can exalt his passion to the level of the divine or invoke Platonic affinities of soul (I.ii.238–9), his speech can also work against this high valuation almost as Putana's does. Of course this is an ambivalence of the culture: in II.i.69–80 the discourse of sex as a coarse joke invades the whole text, in a series of double-entendres not intended by any speaker ('parts I love . . . touch an instrument', etc.). This discourse is now used intermittently in the characterisation of Giovanni. Thus his praise of Annabella's beauty in II.v comes to a climax with

> But father, what is else for pleasure framed,
> Lest I offend your ears, shall go unnamed.   (57–8)

'For pleasure framed' means, of course, framed for men's pleasure, not for her own. Annabella's genitals are suddenly foregrounded as a rib-jogging joke, which is no different from Putana's review of Annabella's suitors in I.ii in terms of their male members. We notice too that this speech, though rapturous in tone, tends to be a catalogue of high-priced possessions (perfumes, jewels, gold thread), as though Annabella were becoming a commodity.[27]

The status of romantic love is questioned again by a different clash of discourses in II.ii. Soranzo, alone and in raptures over thoughts of Annabella and a Petrarchan sonnet, is interrupted by his cast-off mistress, whereupon he switches into very different terms: 'I hate thee and thy lust. You have been too foul' (101). This brutal repudiation of earlier vows not only makes courtly love seem precarious, but questions the social and familial order against which Giovanni and Annabella are pitted, for this is the man to whom the kindly Florio has promised his daughter.

By the end of the scene Hippolita is plotting Soranzo's destruction and Vasques is plotting Hippolita's. Almost the only innocent person in Parma is the 'innocent' Bergetto, who qualifies by being an imbecile; his murder in III.vii achieves unexpected pathos, and brings the Church into prominence as a subject for questioning. Its first representative has been the Friar, a figure of wisdom in I.i, where he gave not only orthodox doctrine but pragmatic advice: fornication is a sin, but a much less grave one than incest; find another girl. In II.v he is still pragmatic: 'Persuade thy sister to some marriage' (40). Morally this advice is more dubious, and it is instantly rejected by Giovanni, in whose eyes Annabella is already married to himself. In III.vi, when Annabella is distraught from finding herself pregnant, the Friar pushes his plan (and Florio's) through by a hell-fire sermon which terrifies her into agreeing to marry Soranzo. His purpose is not merely (as some critics have said) to give Annabella a 'sham respectability', but to buy time for her to achieve true penitence, forgiveness and a better life. His intervention is none the less an ill-judged exercise of priestly power and male authority, and from what we know of Soranzo we expect it to result in disaster. As a concerned and compassionate man the Friar still commands respect.[28] This cannot be said of the Cardinal, who in a speech full of pride and insolence takes the 'nobly born' murderer Grimaldi into the protection of the Pope (III.ix).[29] At this point the moral authority of the Church disappears.

Annabella does not keep (perhaps never intended to keep) her promise to 'leave off this life, and henceforth live to' Soranzo. She continues to be Giovanni's lover, and when Soranzo discovers her pregnancy and beats her, her love and courage are shown in insults to her husband and a defiant refusal to tell her lover's name (IV.iii). This behaviour has been admired by romantic critics, but would have been found less praiseworthy by male playgoers in the seventeenth century: in this middle part of the play Annabella comes to approximate closely to the contemporary stereotype of the bad woman, seen as both lustful and shrewish.[30] Thus her rather childish taunting of Soranzo in the scene of his wooing (III.ii), which might be put down to justified contempt or the high spirits of a woman fulfilled in love, comes to seem of a piece with the 'scurvy looks . . . waspish perverseness and loud fault-finding' she visits on his household after marriage (IV.iii.165–6). Perfect examples are on hand both of the lustful shrew (Hippolita) and the properly submissive woman (Philotis, who after agreeing to love Bergetto, then agrees to retire into a nunnery in the scene before the confrontation between Annabella and Soranzo). Still, we need not assume that all the meanings of the text are sealed within these patriarchal stereotypes, which have themselves been questioned in the play. The comparison with Philotis does not work entirely to Philotis's advantage;[31] and when Annabella is beaten and sadistically threatened for her adultery by a notorious adulterer, the value of the stereotype is changed and her courage may even be admired.

After Annabella's turn to repentance at IV.iii.128–9, the passionate virago disappears and is replaced by a model of sorrowful submission (V.i), even after it must have become clear that the forgiving words by which Soranzo induced her penitence were lies.[32] Giovanni undergoes no such change, and returns to prominence in V.iii still defying 'busy opinion' and also, now, rejecting belief in an after-life. As in the very first scene, his intellectual challenge is undercut as coming from a silly-clever student rationalising his own desires; and those desires oscillate between the idealism of 'united hearts' and the sensual connoisseurship of 'law of sports'. Deflated by the Friar at V.iii.21, he recovers by asserting his heroic will in Tamburlaine-like hyperbolic speech (58–63) which, like some of Tamburlaine's own speeches, is both splendid and absurd. At Soranzo's house in V.v he expects to make love once more, but Annabella rejects him. For him the obvious explanation, unless she has renounced their love for a mere whim (a 'fit', the contemptuous word recalling Putana at II.i.48), is that she has abandoned him for Soranzo. In any case she must die; and after a brief return of tenderness in an exchange full of haunting poetry, he stabs her to the heart, in a savage parody of the sexual act she has denied him.

As he does so he declares 'Revenge is mine; honour doth love command' (V.v.86)—a line originally printed in italic, probably by Ford's direction. 'Revenge is mine' brings into focus the whole revenge ethos and its clash with God's commands, as had been done some thirty years before by Hieronimo's '*Vindicta mihi!*' in Kyd's *The Spanish Tragedy* (III.xiii.1, and cf. Romans xii.19). The line goes on to raise the question of honour, one that much interested Ford. On the title-pages of several late plays (though not of *'Tis Pity*) he placed a motto formed from an anagram of his name, 'Iohn Forde' becoming 'Fide Honor' (Honour through Faith). Faith in the sense of loyalty had always been an essential part of honour; nevertheless the concept was changing during Ford's lifetime, losing the associations with morality given it by Elizabethan definitions, and becoming more a matter of gentlemanly style. Increasingly important elements were sensitivity to insult, promptness to avenge it, and intolerance of rivals in love.[33] Ford was aware of these developments, and introduced a philosopher named Tecnicus into *The Broken Heart* to criticise them: 'real honour / Is the reward of virtue', says Tecnicus, and to murder for revenge is not to win honour but to lose it (III.i.31–51, and cf. IV.i.138–9). Giovanni, a gentleman by education though not by birth, embodies the newer version of honour in an extreme form. Annabella is his love, his wife, and he has lost her to Soranzo; to kill them both is a duty that takes priority over ('doth command') love.

To kill the unfaithful wife was not required by the honour code in north-west Europe at this period, and rarely happened in the English drama; two of the few husbands who do this are Othello, and Caraffa in Ford's *Love's Sacrifice*. But Giovanni is not only maintaining his honour, but keeping faith with the 'past vows and oaths' Annabella has broken, and with their solemn promises to 'Love me, or kill me' at I.ii.254–60. Vows, too, interested Ford as a means of maintaining identity, of achieving what Reid Barbour calls 'the aristocratic virtue of reliable selfhood';[34] and Giovanni is seen from the first to be taking them seriously (II.i.26–7, 32). Unlike the other noble figures in the play, he keeps faith; and when in the next scene he achieves his revenge on Soranzo, he does so without using the treacherous and dishonourable methods of Grimaldo, Richardetto and Soranzo himself. Yet that scene shows him as having performed the most barbarous deed of all.

Annabella has indeed broken faith, and the only defence she could make has already been used and discredited by Soranzo:

> The vows I made, if you remember well,
> Were wicked and unlawful; 'twere more sin
> To keep them than to break them. As for me,
> I cannot mask my penitence.   (II.ii.86–9)

But while Soranzo's love or lust for Hippolita turns into hate, Annabella continues to love Giovanni, though not in the spirit of their vows. Instead of recriminations she speaks the language of affection and concern, and to his 'faithless sister' returns a 'Brother, dear brother'. This kind of loving relationship is of little use to Giovanni: even in the lines, full of pathos and irony, in which he imagines their coming together in an after-life, they must 'do [have sex] as we do here' (V.v.38–41). And his love, like Soranzo's, passes from the possessive to the sadistic; in ripping open Annabella's body in a bizarre literalisation of the familiar metaphor, to 'possess her heart', he does what Soranzo only threatened to do (IV.iii.53–4). In his tyrannical enforcement of their unique marriage vows, he outdoes patriarchy itself.

In the final scene all the elements of the play are brought together and intensified. The public world of Parma is represented by a feast where 'civil mirth' masks fear and hatred, and the intended climax is the murder of Giovanni and the death or disgrace of Annabella in the presence of their father. This world is shattered by Giovanni, whose passion has reached its own climax: the dagger he offered Annabella at I.ii.210 has been used, the pact fulfilled, the link between sex and blood made good. Giovanni's entrance with Annabella's heart on his dagger is sensational, but justified as the logical culmination of a series of speeches in which the deepest truth of a person is located in 'the heart'. The traditional image is sometimes given a physical turn, as at I.ii.211–12 ('Rip up my bosom, there thou shalt behold / A heart in which is writ the truth I speak'), III.ii.23–4, and IV.iii.53–4, but Giovanni presents the corporeal object itself. It can be read in many ways—as a symbol of madness, of destructive possessiveness, of the 'end of lust and pride', even (as Giovanni reads it) of the triumph of love. But perhaps the most powerful shock comes from the fact that this heart appears to signify nothing: it cannot be recognised (V.vi.28), nothing is written on it; the deepest truth of human beings turns out to be a blank, a piece of offal.[35]

The close of the play also questions ideas of Providence. 'Strange miracle of justice!' cries Donado, when Giovanni dies. But divine justice has so often been invoked, and confuted by what we see happening—by Grimaldi when stabbing Bergetto (III.vii.6–7), by Soranzo claiming Annabella as his blessing (IV.i.7–11), by Richardetto the contriver of murder (IV.i.88, IV.ii.8–9)—that such phrases have been emptied of meaning.[36] It is fitting that the Cardinal, a survivor despite Florio's prophecy at III.ix.69–70, should close the play with a few dignified words, after taking care to seize Florio's chattels for 'the Pope's proper use'. His labelling of Annabella as 'a whore' has been anticipated by Soranzo and acted on by Giovanni, but we are unlikely to accept it as coming from his mouth.

As many critics have noted, *'Tis Pity* is like a rewriting of *Romeo and Juliet* in darker colours. Love within the family is far more shocking, more hopelessly star-crossed, than love between feuding families. For Juliet's earthy but loving nurse we have the cynical and careless Putana. For the testy commands of Old Capulet we have the concealed control of Florio. For the decent County Paris we have Soranzo. For Mercutio we have Bergetto. For Prince Escalus we have the Cardinal. The social world of *Romeo and Juliet* is basically an ordered world; that of *'Tis Pity* is one of disorder, self-seeking and hypocrisy, where joy and innocence reside only in an idiot, and we know what kindness and goodness are by the way they are feigned. Thus Florio's genial statement—

> My care is how to match her to her liking;
> I would not have her marry wealth, but love

—gives a pleasant idea of what a father might be, and (as we already know) Florio is not; and a moving speech of Christian forgiveness comes from Soranzo only when he 'carries hell about' him (IV.iii.133–9, 149). Likewise Vasques, a disinterested Machiavel, prostitutes the language of honesty and friendship to purposes of treachery. The nature of ordinary transactions is scarcely concealed by a surface of refinement: Florio's friendly speech to Donado, Donado's pretence that his idiot nephew is sighing like a courtly lover for Annabella (II.vi.7–10), Soranzo's sonnets.

Giovanni and Annabella attempt to construct an alternative inner world, and for a time they succeed. While trust continues between them we do find something like joy and innocence, not only in their first raptures, but in little natural exchanges at coming and going. It comes most touchingly from Annabella: contrast her 'Look you do [return soon]' (II.i.37), the intimate imperative of one lover asking only that the other be there, with Giovanni's authoritarian 'Remember what thou vow'st' (II.i.32). Love gives her a happy assurance, heard in the couplet at II.i.39–40, and in her jokes: 'Tell on' t, y' are best, do'; 'A lusty youth / Signior Donado, gave it me to wear / Against my marriage' (II.i.15, II.vi.135–6). This simple language is reminiscent of the boudoir scene in Webster's *The Duchess of Malfi* (III.ii.1–69), a play Ford admired and for which he wrote a commendatory poem.[37] That Ford should have given it to his incestuous lovers was a victory of the imagination. It is soon superseded by more powerful, more public discourses. Giovanni's speech is finally dominated by the masculine language of possession, command, heroic will (always present in his Tamburlaine vein), and the even harsher language of honour and vengeance, orientated towards death rather than love. Defying the public world to the end, he has already succumbed to it: he and Soranzo are as one. Perhaps this is the real tragedy of the play.

OTHER APPROACHES

More specialised approaches than the one suggested above have been explored. A psychoanalytical reading of Ford's plays may indicate a preoccupation with characters who withhold and deny themselves.[38] The love of Giovanni and Annabella fits this pattern by its narcissistic quality: closely linked by birth and upbringing, sharing 'one beauty' (I.ii.239), in loving each other they are loving themselves. Each (but particularly Giovanni) resists the attempts of the outside world to break into their enclosed space. An incestuous element may be a natural part of the development of sexuality, but failure to transcend it can lead to perversion and even insanity. 'What may look from inside the temple of narcissism like religious mystery and sacrificial rite is seen by the sane who live outside as madness, depravity, monstrous egotism, unnatural lust, and sanguinary dismemberment.'[39] On this view Giovanni's description of Annabella's heart as food on which he feasts (V.vi.24) represents a kind of psychotic cannibalism.[40] Detailed psychoanalysis of imagined characters is a doubtful procedure, but some critics see it as significant that in their original vows, while Annabella invokes 'our mother's dust', Giovanni varies this to 'my mother's dust', as though refusing to share his dead mother even with his sister.[41] Thus his condition may be traced to a primary fixation on the mother, for whom Annabella is a substitute. Without going so far, we might see the mother's absence as important for the close, confined relationship her children have.

Freudian insights also make part of a post-structuralist reading by Susan Wiseman,[42] who notes the absence of any language for incest in the play: the word is seldom used, and sex between siblings is presented in terms of courtly love, or Neoplatonism, or traditional religious discourse. Incest is charged with too many meanings and confuses the categories of nature and culture, family and non-family. (This threat to systems of meaning is related to Derrida's suggestion that conceptual thought was developed expressly to make the origin of the incest taboo unthinkable.)[43] The nearest the text comes to articulating incest directly is at the moment when Annabella's 'secretly familiar' desire for Giovanni comes to the surface in a way that recalls Freud's concept of the 'uncanny' (I.ii.132–6). Otherwise, incest can be read only as confessed to, and constructed by, Putana, the Friar and Vasques. It cannot be read from Annabella's body, which displays pregnancy but not incest; nor from the puzzle of her excavated heart. By categorising Annabella simply as a 'whore', the Cardinal takes the text to safer ground and makes a bid for closure.

In a politicised reading, Terri Clerico[44] tries 'to draw *'Tis Pity* into the mainstream of cultural materialist thought' by insisting that incest is 'a social product', to be related to class antagonisms. Though not an aristocrat, Giovanni resembles Ferdinand in *The Duchess of Malfi* in expressing, through incestuous wishes, a desire for class exclusiveness. His defence of incest as natural attempts to separate nature from culture and suppress (as critics have done) its entanglement in social discourses. The futility of this attempt is shown when Annabella becomes pregnant, which exposes her to 'the speech of the people' (II.i.52) and destroys Florio's social ambitions. These preoccupations are conveyed by the imagery of blood throughout the play, with meanings ranging from 'lineage' to the spattering of Giovanni in V.vi.

Lastly, Ronald Huebert has used 'the lens of the baroque tradition in order to discover Ford the dramatic artist, rather than Ford the rebel, Ford the moralist, or Ford the psychologist'.[45] His plays are not baroque in the sense that the ornate devotional poems of Crashaw are so termed. But his drama is one of grand gestures made against a background of uneasy scepticism—features of the baroque style which dominated the visual arts in the mid-seventeenth century, and may have its counterpart in other arts. More subjective than the Renaissance classicism which preceded it, the baroque style in painting and sculpture finds significance, not in the revelation of order, but in experiences of intense emotion. These experiences tend to fuse together: religious ecstasy is presented in terms of sexual ecstasy and vice versa, and death—perceived as a supreme experience—in terms of both. Perspective and other aspects of representation are distorted for the sake of strong effects, and this art embraces what is extreme, incongruous or paradoxical. Thus the doomed, enclosed love of Giovanni and Annabella combines eroticism and death in a baroque manner in I.ii and again in V.v. (However, the text does not bear out Huebert's view[46] that Annabella dies willingly as one of love's martyrs; such female figures must be found in *Love's Sacrifice* and *The Broken Heart*.) The abrupt reversals in *'Tis Pity*, e.g. of Annabella's role at I.ii.245 and again at IV.iii.128–9, may not be realistic, but neither are they clumsy: they are calculated surprise effects. The spectacular rituals and ceremonies also produce effects allied to the baroque, especially the ritual which solemnises an impossible betrothal in I.ii. All the elements that relate the play to baroque art come to a climax in the final scene.

'Tis Pity was revived at the Restoration, but soon dropped from the repertories; and when interest in the drama of this period was renewed a century later, it was felt that this play presented 'insuperable obstacles to its appearance upon a modern stage'.[47] An adaptation by Maurice Maeterlinck, interestingly titled Annabella, was produced by the Théâtre de l'Oeuvre in Paris in 1894. But it was another thirty years before London productions of 'Tis Pity were given, and then only in 'private performances'—by the Phoenix Society in 1923 and the Arts Theatre Club in 1934. The first public performances since the seventeenth century were given by Donald Wolfit and Company in 1940.

Since then 'Tis Pity has often been produced, both by professional companies and by amateur groups. A film of the play was made in Italy by Giuseppe Patrone Griffi and released in London in 1973 by Miracle Films (with unsatisfactory dubbing); it is now available on video. It departs freely from the text, usually in the spirit of the play and often with imaginative insight; Giovanni's role was played powerfully and obsessively by Oliver Tobias. Radio adaptations were broadcast on the BBC Third Programme in 1962 and on Radio 3 in 1970, and a television version by Roland Joffé on BBC2 in 1980.

Modern productions almost always invite more sympathy for Giovanni and Annabella, as rebels, than would have been likely in the seventeenth century. Accordingly, the Friar has often been rendered as a negative character, sometimes (as in Joffé's 1972 production for the National Theatre) a sadistic one; while full emphasis has been given to the sinister role of the Cardinal, who in Ron Daniels's 1977 RSC production (at the Other Place, Stratford, and the Donmar Warehouse, London) opened the play as well as closed it. Likewise the greed and hypocrisy of bourgeois society has been fully brought out, especially in two productions which set the play in the nineteenth century: the 1977 production by the Actors' Company (directed by Robert Cushman), and Joffé's BBC2 production.

In the earlier revivals the lovers themselves were romanticised; later they were sometimes played as innocents, as in the National Theatre production directed by Alan Ayckbourn in 1988. Generally the emphasis has moved away from romance towards violence and sex: in the 1977 RSC production, II.i opened with the lovers sporting naked in bed. In a production by Philip Prowse for the Citizens'

Theatre, Glasgow, in 1988, Giovanni and Annabella appeared
'charmless and cool'. Critics have often admired sympathetic por-
trayals of Annabella, e.g. by Rosalind Iden in 1940, Zena Walker at
the Mermaid Theatre in 1961, and Cherie Lunghi in the BBC2
production. Actors have tended to play Giovanni as a tormented
neurotic, and have less often been praised. Two productions at least
have emphasised the logic by which their deaths follow on from their
pact, by having Giovanni and Annabella enact their vows in I.ii with
Giovanni's dagger upright between them. These were an earlier
production by the Actors' Company (1974)[48] and an elaborate production by Jerry Turner at the Bowmer Theatre, Oregon, in 1981.

The sub-plots with Hippolita, Richardetto, Bergetto and
Grimaldi were eliminated from Maeterlinck's *Annabella* and Griffi's
film. Where retained, they have sometimes baffled and annoyed
reviewers but sometimes worked well. Bergetto's part, often dispar-
aged by critics, can be made very funny and finally moving, as it was
by Harold Scott in 1923 and 1934; great pathos was achieved by the
death of Bergetto and the grief of the loyal Poggio in two RSC
productions, Ron Daniels's of 1977 and David Leveaux's at the
Swan in 1991. In 1977 the RSC made the dialogue in which
Richardetto consigns Philotis to a nunnery (IV.ii) more impressive
by staging it in candlelight over Hippolita's body. In the BBC2
production Bergetto and Philotis were allowed to elope in a stage-
coach. Vasques's banditti have appeared as *mafiosi*.

A director must often resolve questions that the text leaves unan-
swered. Usually Annabella's first repentance, in III.vi, has been
played as genuine; but the Oregon production showed her giving no
real weight, at this stage, to the Friar's words, and the scene was
omitted from Griffi's film. In that film the problem of how
Giovanni, a possessive lover, can tolerate sharing Annabella with
Soranzo for some months was solved by having Annabella refuse to
consummate their marriage, until eventually Soranzo succeeds in
arousing her desire; so that Giovanni's accusation at V.v.1–5 is true.
In V.v it is not clear whether Annabella fully realises that Giovanni
is going to kill her. In the 1977 RSC production she was afraid and
confused, playing to 'What means this?' (V.v.83). In the BBC2
production she not only expected it, but agreed to it as part of their
pact, offering him a cut-throat razor and her wrists.

The most difficult moment to produce has always been
Giovanni's entry at V.vi.10 with Annabella's heart on his dagger.
The heart would not be easily recognised as such in a large modern

theatre,[49] but nor would it have been in the candlelit Phoenix or at the Red Bull. The audience must have been left to guess what has happened from Giovanni's words and blood-splashed appearance until he tells them explicitly twenty lines after his entrance. Slow revelation is probably best; otherwise the shock effect is so strong and grotesque that the audience may recoil into laughter.[50] In the Phoenix Society production the heart was omitted altogether. In the 1977 RSC production Giovanni held the heart in his gloved hand. For the Oregon production a prop was devised combining in appearance both heart and dagger; the heart was at first covered by a cloth, then gradually revealed.

FURTHER READING

The most useful one-volume collection of plays by Ford is *'Tis Pity She's a Whore' and Other Plays*, ed. Marion Lomax (Oxford: Oxford University Press, World's Classics, 1995), in which the other plays are *The Lover's Melancholy*, *The Broken Heart* and *Perkin Warbeck*. *John Ford: Three Plays*, ed. Keith Sturgess (Harmondsworth: Penguin, 1970) contains *'Tis Pity*, *The Broken Heart* and *Perkin Warbeck*. All these plays have been edited for the Revels Plays and other series, but there is still no good modern edition of one major play, *Love's Sacrifice*. *The Fancies Chaste and Noble* and *The Lady's Trial* may be found in Alexander Dyce's edition of the *Works* (3 vols, 1869). *The Witch of Edmonton* is included in *Three Jacobean Witchcraft Plays*, ed. Peter Corbin and Douglas Sedge (Manchester: Manchester University Press, Revels Companion Library, 1986). Poems and prose pieces are collected in *The Nondramatic Works of John Ford*, ed. L. E. Stock *et al.* (Binghamton, NY: Center for Medieval and Early Renaissance Studies, 1991).

The best introductory book is now Rowland Wymer, *Webster and Ford*,[51] which has an excellent chapter on 'Ford and Caroline Theatre' and a chapter on *'Tis Pity* that keeps staging in view. A good collection of essays is *'Concord in Discord'*, ed. Donald K. Anderson, Jr, and an even better one is *John Ford: Critical Re-Visions*, ed. Michael Neill. *Professional Dramatists*, by Ira Clark, has an exceptionally clear and well-documented chapter on Ford, though he exaggerates Ford's gentlemanly conservatism and has less to say on *'Tis Pity* than on *The Broken Heart*. There is a close and well-balanced reading of *'Tis Pity* in John S. Wilks, *The Idea of Conscience in Renaissance Tragedy* (London and New York: Routledge, 1990), chapter 10. In *John Ford's Political Theatre*, Lisa Hopkins is informative about Ford's dedicatees and discusses the theme of food and poison in *'Tis Pity*. Earlier studies that still have value include G. F. Sensabaugh, *The Tragic Muse of John Ford* (Stanford, CA: Stanford University Press, 1944), for Ford the romantic rebel; Clifford Leech, *John Ford and the Drama of his Time* (London: Chatto & Windus, 1957), especially for the Jacobean elements in *'Tis Pity*; and Mark Stavig, *John Ford and the Traditional Moral Order* (Madison: University of Wisconsin Press, 1968), interpreting Ford as an orthodox moralist.

Incest in the life, thought and literature of the age is fully explored by Richard A. McCabe in *Incest, Drama and Nature's Law, 1550–1700*; also by Charles R. Forker in his long essay ' "A Little More than Kin" '. The first two chapters of Robin Fox, *The Red Lamp of Incest* (London: Hutchinson, 1980) give a lively, open-minded survey of theories of the incest taboo and the forms it takes in different societies.

On matters of critical theory raised by *'Tis Pity*, the concept of the 'interrogative text', first put forward by Emile Benveniste, is outlined by Catherine Belsey in *Critical Practice* (London: Methuen, 1980), pp. 90–102, and applied, e.g. to *Dr Faustus*, by Jonathan Dollimore in *Radical Tragedy: Religion, Ideology and Power in the Drama of Shakespeare and his Contemporaries* (New York and London: Harvester Wheatsheaf, 2nd edn, 1989). Other basic issues are discussed by Belsey in *The Subject of Tragedy*. See also *Rewriting the Renaissance: The Discourses of Sexual Difference in Early Modern Europe*, ed. Margaret W. Ferguson, Maureen Quilligan and Nancy J. Vickers (Chicago: University of Chicago Press, 1986), especially Jonathan Goldberg's chapter 'Fatherly Authority: The Politics of Stuart Family Images'. For 'cultural materialism', see *New Historicism and Renaissance Drama*, ed. Richard Wilson and Richard Dutton (London and New York: Longman, 1992).

For the drama of the period generally, see *The Revels History of Drama in English*, vol. 6: 1613–1660, ed. Philip Edwards *et al.* (London: Methuen, 1981); Marion Lomax, *Stage Images and Traditions: Shakespeare to Ford* (Cambridge: Cambridge University Press, 1987); Andrew Gurr, *Playgoing in Shakespeare's London*; and *The Cambridge Companion to English Renaissance Drama*, ed. A. R. Braunmuller and Michael Hattaway (Cambridge: Cambridge University Press, 1990), especially Robert N. Watson's chapter on 'Tragedy' and James Bulman's on 'Caroline Drama'. Lastly, two stories which may not throw much light on the play but are fun: William Golding's 'The Scorpion God', in the volume of that title (London: Faber, 1971) describes a kingdom in pre-Pharaonic Egypt in which sex is considered gravely immoral unless the partners are closely related by blood; and Angela Carter's 'John Ford's *'Tis Pity She's a Whore*', in *American Ghosts and Old World Wonders* (London: Chatto & Windus, 1993) outlines a treatment for a film by John Ford, the director of westerns.

NOTES

1 Unless otherwise specified, sources for statements in this section are given in the Revels edition of *'Tis Pity* (1975), pp. xix–xxvi, xxxvii–xxxix.

2 Martin Butler, 'The Connection between Donne, Clarendon, and Ford', *Notes & Queries*, 34 (1987), 309–10.

3 Ira Clark, *Professional Playwrights: Massinger, Ford, Shirley and Brome* (Lexington: University Press of Kentucky, 1992), p. 75.

4 Lisa Hopkins, *John Ford's Political Theatre* (Manchester: Manchester University Press, 1994), esp. pp. 45–8. See also Brian Manning, 'The Aristocracy and the Downfall of Charles I', in Manning, ed. *Politics, Religion and the English Civil War* (London: Edward Arnold, 1973), pp. 35–80, esp. pp. 37–41.

5 *Webster and Ford* (London and New York: St Martin's Press, 1995), p. 96.

6 Verna Foster, ' *'Tis Pity She's a Whore* as City Tragedy', in *John Ford: Critical Re-Visions*, ed. Michael Neill (Cambridge: Cambridge University Press, 1988), pp. 181–200. For arguments in favour of an early date see the Revels edition, pp. xxxvii–xli.

7 Hopkins, p. 28.

8 See Beatrice White, *Cast of Ravens: The Strange Case of Sir Thomas Overbury* (London: John Murray, 1965).

9 The story was false, and may or may not have reached Ford before he wrote *'Tis Pity*. See Lisa Hopkins, 'A Source for John Ford's *'Tis Pity She's a Whore*', *Notes & Queries*, 41 (1994), 520–1.

10 See David M. Bergeron, 'Brother–Sister Relationships in Ford's 1633 Plays', in *'Concord in Discord': The Plays of John Ford, 1586–1986*, ed. Donald K. Anderson, Jr (New York: AMS Press, 1986), pp. 195–219.

11 For details about the Phoenix see John Orrell, *The Theatres of Inigo Jones and John Webb* (Cambridge: Cambridge University Press, 1985), chapter 3; Keith Sturgess, *Jacobean Private Theatre* (London: Routledge & Kegan Paul, 1987), chapter 3. Inigo Jones's plans are reproduced in both books and Sturgess includes a photograph of a model.

12 For the audience of the private theatres see Martin Butler, *Theatre and Crisis 1632–1642* (Cambridge: Cambridge University Press, 1984), chapter 6; Sturgess, chapter 2; Andrew Gurr, *Playgoing in Shakespeare's London* (Cambridge: Cambridge University Press, 1987), chapters 3 and 4.

13 Gurr, pp. 170–7.

14 Gurr, p. 177.

15 Unrelated persons brought up in the same children's group of a kibbutz avoid sexual partnerships later. See Melford E. Spiro, *Children of the Kibbutz* (New York: Schocken Books, 1965), pp. 326–35, 347–9.

16 F. G. Emmison, *Elizabethan Life: Morals and the Church Courts* (Chelmsford: Essex County Council, 1973), pp. 36–8, citing unpublished research by A. D. J. Macfarlane.

17 Sigmund Freud, *Totem and Taboo* (1913), trans. James Strachey (London: Routledge & Kegan Paul, 1950). The reformulation by Claude Lévi-Strauss in *The Elementary Structures of Kinship* (trans. James Harle, Boston, MA: Beacon Press, 1969) is less specifically sexual and gives more importance to cultural factors, especially language, but accounts for the supposedly universal 'horror' in much the same way; in his view it functions to ensure exogamy.

18 Karen C. Meiselman, *Incest: A Psychological Study of Causes and Effects* (San Francisco: Jossey-Bass, 1984), chapters 7–8, esp. pp. 263–74; the samples are small. See also Herbert Maisch, *Incest*, trans. Colin Bearne (London: André Deutsch, 1973), pp. 205–6.

19 An exception is that of ancient Egypt, which 'sanctioned full brother-sister marriage for all social classes'; see Luciano M. Santiago, *The Children of Oedipus: Brother–Sister Incest in Psychiatry, Literature, History and Mythology* (New York: Libra, 1973), chapter 1 and p. 174.

20 Richard A. McCabe, *Incest, Drama and Nature's Law, 1550–1700* (Cambridge: Cambridge University Press, 1993), p. 33.

21 Hugo Grotius, *De jure belli ac pacis* (1625), cited from the 1655 English translation in Robert Ornstein, *The Moral Vision of Jacobean Tragedy* (Madison: University of Wisconsin Press, 1960), p. 207.

22 This argument appears in Aristotle and Aquinas (see Jack Goody, *The Development of the Family and Marriage in Europe* (Cambridge: Cambridge University Press, 1983), pp. 57–8), and in Montaigne's essay 'Of Moderation' (trans. by John Florio in 1603).

23 Arthur Lake, *Sermons with some Religious Meditations* (1629), quoted by McCabe, p. 14.

24 Lawrence Stone, *The Family, Sex and Marriage in England 1500–1800* (London: Weidenfeld & Nicolson, 1977), p. 115.

25 For one critic this lie is crucial: 'Not until her brother authorizes thinking about incest by claiming that both "wise Nature" (I.ii.236) and "holy Church" (I.ii.241) approve does [Annabella] tell him how she feels'. Nathaniel Strout, 'The Tragedy of Annabella in *'Tis Pity She's a Whore*', in *Traditions and Innovations: Essays on British Literature of the Middle Ages and the Renaissance*, ed. David G. Allen and Robert A. White (Newark, NJ: University of Delaware Press, 1990), pp. 163–76 (p. 170).

26 The real-life Frances Coke proved less docile than Philotis in 1617, when her father, a former Lord Chief Justice, counselled her to marry the mentally unstable brother of James I's favourite; she had to be compelled to it by force. For the fullest account see Antonia Fraser, *The Weaker Vessel: Woman's Lot in Seventeenth-century England* (London: Weidenfeld & Nicolson, 1984), pp. 12–20.

27 It was logical of Ford's first editor, Robert Dodsley, to amend 'colour' in 51 to 'coral'. The catalogue resembles several discussed by Laura Brown in *Alexander Pope* (Oxford: Blackwell, 1985) in terms of the Marxian concept of 'commodification'.

28 Critics disagree sharply in their judgement of the Friar. For a good discussion see Gilles D. Montsarrat, 'The Unity of John Ford: *'Tis Pity She's a Whore* and *Christ's Bloody Sweat*', *Studies in Philology*, 77 (1980), 247–70, esp. 249–55. Montsarrat distinguishes firmly between the Friar, who represents Christianity, and the Cardinal, who represents only the Pope.

29 This scene had a detailed real-life counterpart in the action of the Papal Nuncio at Venice, in 1607, to protect Ridolfi Poma and his accomplices after their attempt to murder Paolo Sarpi; see Revels Plays edition, pp. xxxv–xxxvi.

30 Lisa Jardine, *Still Harping on Daughters: Women and Drama in the Age of Shakespeare* (New York and London: Harvester Wheatsheaf, 2nd edition, [1989]), p. 104. Jardine shows the connection perceived between women's scolding, or even talking, and lust.

31 George C. Herndl sees Philotis as a satire on the ideals of 'the respectable world' (*The High Design: English Renaissance Tragedy and the Natural Law* (Lexington: University Press of Kentucky, 1970), p. 266). But for Hopkins she is the 'dispenser of real food and genuine comfort' (*John Ford's Political Theatre*, p. 84).

32 This disjunction between phases of a dramatic character, each corresponding to a female sterotype, is what Catherine Belsey finds in the role of Vittoria in Webster's *The White Devil*; she relates it to the fact that in contemporary discourses about women, controlled by men, women were 'only inconsistently identified as subjects'. See *The Subject of Tragedy: Identity and Difference in Renaissance Drama* (London: Methuen, 1985, repr. Routledge, 1993), pp. 160–4. But Strout reads Annabella as a consistent character, always strongly influenced by deference towards males.

33 C. L. Barber, *The Idea of Honour in the English Drama, 1591–1700* (Göteborg: University of Göteborg, 1957), esp. pp. 272–9; Mervyn James, 'English Politics and the Concept of Honour, 1485–1642', in James, *Society, Politics and Culture: Studies in Early Modern England* (Cambridge: Cambridge University Press, 1986), pp. 308–415.

34 'John Ford and Resolve', *Studies in Philology*, 86 (1989), 341–66 (p. 345); the article discusses 'vows' as a short-lived literary genre and a way of defending aristocratic conceptions of life in troubled times.

35 See Michael Neill, ' "What Strange Riddle's This?" Deciphering *'Tis Pity She's a Whore*', in Neill, ed. *John Ford: Critical Re-Visions* (cited above, n. 6), pp. 153–79.

36 As noted by Richard C. Ide, 'Ford's *'Tis Pity She's a Whore* and the Benefits of Belatedness', in Anderson, ed. *'Concord in Discord'* (cited above, n. 10), pp. 61–86.

37 Neill compares this scene from *The Duchess* with Giovanni's wooing of Annabella in I.ii, suggesting that 'Ford learned to write the spare, broken dialogue, stumbling between prose and irregular verse' from Webster (' "What Strange Riddle's This?" ', pp. 169–71).

38 William D. Dyer, 'Holding/Withholding Environments: A Psychoanalytic Approach to Ford's *The Broken Heart*', *English Literary Renaissance*, 21 (1991), 401–24.

39 Charles R. Forker, ' "A Little More than Kin, and Less than Kind": Incest, Intimacy, Narcissism, and Identity in Elizabethan and Stuart Drama', *Medieval & Renaissance Drama in England*, 4 (1989), 13–51 (p. 43). Blair and Rita Justice discuss one type of incest as a form of elitism, between siblings who 'get the idea that they are too good for the rest of the world': see *The Broken Taboo: Sex in the Family* (New York and London: Human Sciences Press, 1980), p. 75.

40 Richard Marienstras, 'Incest and Social Relations in *'Tis Pity She's a Whore* by John Ford', in Marienstras, *New Perspectives on the Shakesperian World*, trans. Janet Lloyd (Cambridge: Cambridge University Press, 1985), chapter 8 (p. 200).

41 Marienstras, p. 195. For Marienstras 'the incest, followed by the assassination of Annabella, is a means of killing the father' (p. 195).

42 Wiseman, ' *'Tis Pity She's a Whore*': Representing the Incestuous Body', in *Renaissance Bodies: The Human Figure in English Culture c. 1540–1660*, ed. Lucy Gent and Nigel Llewellyn (London: Reaktion Books, 1990), pp. 180–97.

43 Wiseman refers to Jacques Derrida, 'Structure, Sign and Play', in his *Writing and Difference*, trans. Alan Bass (London: Routledge, 1978), p. 284; cf. also Claude Lévi-Strauss in *Structural Anthropology* (New York: Basic Books, 1963).

44 Clerico, 'The Politics of Blood: John Ford's *'Tis Pity She's a Whore*', *English Literary Renaissance*, 22 (1992), 405–34.

45 Huebert, *John Ford: Baroque English Dramatist* (Montreal and London: McGill-Queen's University Press, 1977), p. 34. Some effects involving surprise and incongruity might better be termed 'mannerist': see Huebert, pp. 14–19, and discussions of mannerism cited by Michael Neill in '"Wits Most Accomplished Senate": The Audience of the Caroline Private Theaters', *Studies in English Literature*, 18 (1978), 341–60 (p. 359).

46 Huebert, pp. 54–5, 76.

47 Sources for most statements and quotations in this section are given in the Revels edition of *'Tis Pity* (1975), pp. lvii–lxii, or in one of the following essays: Alan C. Dessen, '*'Tis Pity She'a Whore*: Modern Productions and the Scholar', in Anderson, ed. *'Concord in Discord'*, pp. 87–108; Roger Warren, 'Ford in Performance', in Neill, ed. *John Ford: Critical Re-Visions*, pp. 11–27, esp. pp. 12–19. Some details of productions since 1988 are taken from Wymer, *Webster and Ford*, chapter 8, and *''Tis Pity She's a Whore' and Other Plays*, ed. Marion Lomax (Oxford: Oxford University Press, World's Classics, 1995), pp. xvi–xix.

48 See A. P. Hogan, '*'Tis Pity She's a Whore*: The Overall Design', *Studies in English Literature*, 17 (1977), 303–16 (p. 307).

49 See Nicholas Brooke, *Horrid Laughter in Jacobean Tragedy* (London: Open Books, 1979), p. 124. Brooke reports the use of 'a large cardboard heart' to make recognition easier.

50 For examples of this effect see Dessen, pp. 89–90; Hogan, p. 310n. As Brooke shows, an element of the absurd is intrinsic to this 'brilliant but difficult climax' (*Horrid Laughter*, pp. 124–5).

51 Where a full reference is not given, the work has already been cited in these notes.

'TIS PITY
SHE'S A WHORE

[THE EPISTLE]

To the truly noble, John, Earl of Peterborough, Lord
Mordaunt, Baron of Turvey.

My Lord,

Where a truth of merit hath a general warrant, there love is
but a debt, acknowledgement a justice. Greatness cannot   5
often claim virtue by inheritance; yet in this yours appears
most eminent, for that you are not more rightly heir to your
fortunes than glory shall be to your memory. Sweetness of
disposition ennobles a freedom of birth; in both, your lawful
interest adds honour to your own name, and mercy to my   10
presumption. Your noble allowance of these first fruits of my
leisure in the action emboldens my confidence of your as
noble construction in this presentment; especially since my
service must ever owe particular duty to your favours, by a
particular engagement. The gravity of the subject may easily   15

[The Epistle]

1–2.] John Mordaunt (c. 1599–1643) came of an old Catholic family,
disgraced by his father's alleged involvement in the Gunpowder Plot.
Mordaunt nevertheless found favour under James, was converted to Protestantism in 1625, and was created first Earl of Peterborough in 1628. Nothing
is known about his relations with Ford beyond this obscurely-worded dedication.

4. *Where . . . warrant*] 'where there is every reason for believing that a man
has true merit'.

9. *ennobles*] raises the status already conferred by.

freedom of birth] gentle birth.

9–10. *lawful interest*] rightful claim.

11. *allowance*] approval.

11–12. *first fruits of my leisure*] This may mean that *'Tis Pity* was the first
play Ford had written or would acknowledge, or that it was written during a
period of leisure that Peterborough knew about.

12. *in the action*] in performance; the production Peterborough had approved need not have been the first one.

12–13. *emboldens . . . presentment*] 'makes me believe that you will be as
generous in accepting this dedication'. *Presentment* also suggests dramatic
performance.

15. *engagement*] obligation. The obvious interpretation is that Peterborough, who had married an heiress in 1625, had given Ford some financial
assistance.

excuse the lightness of the title; otherwise I had been a severe judge against mine own guilt. Princes have vouchsafed grace to trifles, offered from a purity of devotion; your lordship may likewise please to admit into your good opinion, with these weak endeavours, the constancy of affection from the sincere 20 lover of your deserts in honour,

JOHN FORD.

---

16. *lightness*] frivolity. ' 'Tis pity' leads one to expect something not too serious, like 'she has bad breath', and Ford's title may have been a catch-phrase used facetiously, e.g. in reply to praise of a woman's beauty.

To my Friend, the Author.

With admiration I beheld this Whore
Adorned with beauty, such as might restore
(If ever being as thy Muse hath famed)
Her Giovanni, in his love unblamed.   5
The ready Graces lent their willing aid;
Pallas herself now played the chamber-maid
And helped to put her dressings on. Secure
Rest thou, that thy name herein shall endure
To th' end of age; and Annabella be   10
Gloriously fair, even in her infamy.

THOMAS ELLICE.

[To my Friend, the Author]
This commendatory poem appears in some copies of the 1633 edition. Thomas Ellice and his brother Robert (one of the dedicatees of *The Lover's Melancholy*) were members of Gray's Inn, along with Ford's cousin and namesake. For their literary circle see Mary Hobbs, 'Robert and Thomas Ellice, Friends of Ford and Davenant', *Notes & Queries*, 21 (1974), 292–3.

2. *admiration*] wonder.

4. *famed*] reported.

6. *Graces*] three daughters of Zeus, givers of beauty, grace and kindness.

7. *Pallas*] a goddess identified with Athene and Minerva, patron of all the arts.

8. *dressings*] Since 'this Whore' is a metonymy for Ford's play, 'her dressings' (garments) may be the additional beauties conferred in the stage production.

The Scene

PARMA

The Actors' Names:

BONAVENTURA, *a friar.*
A Cardinal, *nuncio to the Pope.* 5
SORANZO, *a nobleman.*
FLORIO, *a citizen of Parma.*
DONADO, *another citizen.*
GRIMALDI, *a Roman gentleman.*
GIOVANNI, *son to Florio.* 10
BERGETTO, *nephew to Donado.*
RICHARDETTO, *a supposed physician.*
VASQUES, *servant to Soranzo.*
POGGIO, *servant to Bergetto.*
Banditti. 15
[Officers.
Attendants.]

Women:

ANNABELLA, *daughter to Florio.*
HIPPOLITA, *wife to Richardetto.* 20
PHILOTIS, *his niece.*
PUTANA, *tutress to Annabella.*
[Ladies.]

[The Actors' Names]
Most of these names are those of authors (e.g. John Florio, whose *First Fruits* Ford had been reading), or characters in the literature of the day. *Putana* means 'whore'. *Giovanni* is pronounced throughout with four syllables.

'Tis Pity She's a Whore

[Act I]

[I. i]

Enter Friar and GIOVANNI.

Friar. Dispute no more in this, for know, young man,
    These are no school-points. Nice philosophy
    May tolerate unlikely arguments,
    But heaven admits no jest; wits that presumed
    On wit too much, by striving how to prove   5
    There was no God, with foolish grounds of art,
    Discovered first the nearest way to hell,
    And filled the world with devilish atheism.
    Such questions, youth, are fond; for better 'tis
    To bless the sun than reason why it shines;   10
    Yet he thou talk'st of is above the sun—
    No more! I may not hear it.
Giovanni.   Gentle father,
    To you I have unclasped my burdened soul,
    Emptied the storehouse of my thoughts and heart,
    Made myself poor of secrets; have not left   15
    Another word untold, which hath not spoke

I.i.2. *school-points*] questions for theological students to debate as exercises.

Nice] fond of making fine distinctions.

4. *admits*] allows.

wits] thinkers, men of learning.

5. *wit*] human intelligence.

6. *grounds of art*] methods of reasoning.

7. *nearest*] shortest.

9. *fond*] foolish.

11. *he*] God.

32

All what I ever durst or think, or know;
And yet is here the comfort I shall have?
Must I not do what all men else may—love?
Friar. Yes, you may love, fair son.
Giovanni.   Must I not praise   20
That beauty which, if framed anew, the gods
Would make a god of if they had it there,
And kneel to it, as I do kneel to them?
Friar. Why, foolish madman!
Giovanni.   Shall a peevish sound,
A customary form, from man to man,   25
Of brother and of sister, be a bar
'Twixt my perpetual happiness and me?
Say that we had one father, say one womb
(Curse to my joys!) gave both us life and birth;
Are we not therefore each to other bound   30
So much the more by nature? By the links
Of blood, of reason? Nay, if you will have 't,
Even of religion, to be ever one,
One soul, one flesh, one love, one heart, one *all*?
Friar. Have done, unhappy youth, for thou art lost!   35
Giovanni. Shall then, for that I am her brother born,
My joys be ever banished from her bed?
No, father; in your eyes I see the change
Of pity and compassion; from your age,
As from a sacred oracle, distils   40
The life of counsel. Tell me, holy man,
What cure shall give me ease in these extremes?
Friar. Repentance, son, and sorrow for this sin;
For thou hast moved a Majesty above
With thy unrangèd almost blasphemy.   45

---

17. *All what*] all that.
24. *peevish*] (a) senseless; (b) spiteful.
25. *A customary . . . to man*] a purely human convention.
35. *Have done*] stop, be silent.
unhappy] unfortunate.
36. *for that*] because.
40. *oracle*] source of supernatural guidance.
41. *life of counsel*] essence of wise judgement.
45. *unrangèd almost blasphemy*] either 'uncontrolled near-blasphemy' or 'almost limitless blasphemy'.

Giovanni. O, do not speak of that, dear confessor.
Friar. Art thou, my son, that miracle of wit
  Who once, within these three months, wert esteemed
  A wonder of thine age, throughout Bononia?
  How did the university applaud   50
  Thy government, behaviour, learning, speech,
  Sweetness, and all that could make up a man!
  I was proud of my tutelage, and chose
  Rather to leave my books than part with thee;
  I did so—but the fruits of all my hopes   55
  Are lost in thee, as thou art in thyself.
  O Giovanni! Hast thou left the schools
  Of knowledge, to converse with lust and death?
  For death waits on thy lust. Look through the world,
  And thou shalt see a thousand faces shine   60
  More glorious than this idol thou adorest.
  Leave her, and take thy choice; 'tis much less sin,
  Though in such games as those they lose that win.
Giovanni. It were more ease to stop the ocean
  From floats and ebbs, than to dissuade my vows. 65
Friar. Then I have done, and in thy wilful flames
  Already see thy ruin. Heaven is just;
  Yet hear my counsel.
Giovanni.   As a voice of life.
Friar. Hie to thy father's house, there lock thee fast
  Alone within thy chamber, then fall down   70
  On both thy knees, and grovel on the ground;
  Cry to thy heart, wash every word thou utter'st
  In tears, and, if 't be possible, of blood;
  Beg heaven to cleanse the leprosy of lust
  That rots thy soul; acknowledge what thou art, 75

---

46. *confessor*] stressed on the first syllable.
49. *Bononia*] Bologna.
51. *government*] discretion.
53. *tutelage*] guardianship.
55. *I did so*] I gave up my post at Bologna for your sake.
65. *floats and ebbs*] flowing and ebbing.
vows] desires.
68. *voice of life*] (a) life-giving voice; (b) voice from heaven.
69. *Hie*] go quickly.
73. *tears . . . of blood*] tears expressing grief from the heart.

A wretch, a worm, a nothing; weep, sigh, pray
Three times a day, and three times every night.
For seven days' space do this, then if thou find'st
No change in thy desires, return to me;
I'll think on remedy. Pray for thyself   80
At home, whilst I pray for thee here. Away!
My blessing with thee; we have need to pray.
Giovanni. All this I'll do, to free me from the rod
Of vengeance; else I'll swear my fate's my god.

Exeunt.

[I. ii]

Enter GRIMALDI *and* VASQUES *ready to fight.*

Vasques. Come, sir, stand to your tackling; if you prove craven I'll make you run quickly.
Grimaldi. Thou art no equal match for me.
Vasques. Indeed, I never went to the wars to bring home
news, nor cannot play the mountebank for a meal's meat,   5
and swear I got my wounds in the field. See you these
grey hairs? They'll not flinch for a bloody nose. Wilt thou
to this gear?
Grimaldi. Why, slave, think'st thou I'll balance my reputation
with a cast-suit? Call thy master, he shall know that I   10
dare—
Vasques. Scold like a cot-quean, that's your profession. Thou
poor shadow of a soldier, I will make thee know my
master keeps servants thy betters in quality and performance. Com'st thou to fight, or prate?   15

I.ii.1. *tackling*] weapons.

1–2. *craven*] a coward.

3. *equal*] socially equal. By the honour code one gentleman was obliged to
fight another in a duel if challenged, but Grimaldi can claim that to fight with
Vasques, a servant, would degrade him.

5. *mountebank*] self-advertising impostor.

for a meal's meat] to be given a meal.

8. *gear*] business (of fighting).

10. *cast-suit*] servant, wearer of cast-off clothes.

12. *cot-quean*] abusive lower-class woman.

14. *quality*] (a) birth; (b) character.

15. *prate*] chatter.

Grimaldi. Neither, with thee. I am a Roman and a gentleman,
   one that have got mine honour with expense of blood.
Vasques. You are a lying coward and a fool; fight, or by these
   hilts I'll kill thee. [*Grimaldi draws.*] Brave my lord! You'll
   fight?   20
Grimaldi. Provoke me not, for if thou dost—
Vasques. Have at you!   *They fight; Grimaldi hath the worst.*

                Enter FLORIO, DONADO, SORANZO.

Florio. What mean these sudden broils so near my doors?
   Have you not other places but my house
   To vent the spleen of your disordered bloods?   25
   Must I be haunted still with such unrest
   As not to eat or sleep in peace at home?
   Is this your love, Grimaldi? Fie, 'tis naught.
Donado. And Vasques, I may tell thee 'tis not well
   To broach these quarrels; you are ever forward   30
   In seconding contentions.

             Enter above ANNABELLA *and* PUTANA.

Florio.   What's the ground?
Soranzo. That, with your patience, signiors, I'll resolve.
   This gentleman, whom fame reports a soldier—
   For else I know not—rivals me in love
   To Signior Florio's daughter; to whose ears   35
   He still prefers his suit, to my disgrace,

---

   19. *Brave my lord!*] either (a) 'Do you dare to challenge my master,
Soranzo?' or, ironically to Grimaldi when he prepares to fight, (b) 'This is
brave of you!'
   23. *broils*] quarrels.
   25. *spleen*] organ whose secretions were thought to cause anger.
   26. *still*] always.
   28. *naught*] (a) worthless; (b) badly behaved.
   31. *seconding*] stirring up.
   ground] cause of dispute.
   31. S.D. Enter above] i.e. on the upper stage, where they can see and hear
without being observed.
   32. *resolve*] explain.
   34. *For . . . not*] i.e. 'for I have no other evidence than report, that he is a
soldier'.
   36. *prefers*] proffers, presses.

Thinking the way to recommend himself
Is to disparage me in his report.
But know, Grimaldi, though may be thou art
My equal in thy blood, yet this bewrays   40
A lowness in thy mind; which, wert thou noble,
Thou wouldst as much disdain as I do thee
For this unworthiness; and on this ground
I willed my servant to correct thy tongue,
Holding a man so base no match for me.   45

Vasques. And had not your sudden coming prevented us, I
had let my gentleman blood under the gills; I should have
wormed you, sir, for running mad.

Grimaldi. I'll be revenged, Soranzo.

Vasques. On a dish of warm broth to stay your stomach—do,   50
honest innocence, do! Spoon-meat is a wholesomer diet
than a Spanish blade.

Grimaldi. Remember this!

Soranzo.   I fear thee not, Grimaldi.

Exit GRIMALDI.

Florio. My lord Soranzo, this is strange to me,
Why you should storm, having my word engaged.   55
Owing her heart, what need you doubt her ear?
Losers may talk by law of any game.

Vasques. Yet the villainy of words, Signior Florio, may be
such as would make any unspleened dove choleric.
Blame not my lord in this.   60

Florio. Be you more silent.
I would not for my wealth my daughter's love

---

40. *bewrays*] reveals.

47. *gills*] flesh under the jaws and ears, where the blood was supposed to
rise in anger.

48. *wormed*] To worm a dog was to cut a small ligament in its tongue to
prevent rabies.

for running mad] (a) to prevent your going mad; (b) to cure you of anger.

50. *stay your stomach*] (a) satisfy your appetite; (b) lower your pride.

51. *honest innocence*] good, harmless creature.

Spoon-meat] soft or liquid food for the sick or toothless.

56. *Owing*] owning.

57. *Losers may talk*] a proverb: one who has lost, in this case Grimaldi, may
be allowed the satisfaction of grumbling.

59. *unspleened dove*] cf. 25, above.

Should cause the spilling of one drop of blood.
Vasques, put up, let's end this fray in wine.

    Exeunt [FLORIO, DONADO, SORANZO *and* VASQUES].

Putana. How like you this, child? Here's threat'ning, chal-   65
    lenging, quarrelling and fighting on every side, and all is
    for your sake. You had need look to yourself, charge;
    you'll be stol'n away sleeping else shortly.

Annabella. But tutress, such a life gives no content
    To me; my thoughts are fixed on other ends.   70
    Would you would leave me.

Putana. Leave you? No marvel else; leave me no leaving,
    charge, this is love outright. Indeed I blame you not; you
    have choice fit for the best lady in Italy.

Annabella. Pray do not talk so much.   75

Putana. Take the worst with the best, there's Grimaldi the
    soldier, a very well-timbered fellow; they say he is a
    Roman, nephew to the Duke Mount Ferratto; they say he
    did good service in the wars against the Millanoys—but
    faith, charge, I do not like him, an 't be for nothing but   80
    for being a soldier; one amongst twenty of your skirmish-
    ing captains but have some privy maim or other that mars
    their standing upright. I like him the worse he crinkles so
    much in the hams; though he might serve if there were no
    more men, yet he's not the man I would choose.   85

Annabella. Fie, how thou prat'st.

Putana. As I am a very woman, I like Signior Soranzo well.
    He is wise, and what is more, rich; and what is more than
    that, kind; and what is more than all this, a nobleman;
    such a one, were I the fair Annabella myself, I would wish   90
    and pray for. Then he is bountiful; besides he is hand-

---

64. *put up*] sheathe your sword.

67. *charge*] person in my charge.

72. *No marvel else*] i.e. 'of course that's what you'd like'.

leave . . . leaving] i.e. 'don't talk to me about leaving you'.

77. *well-timbered*] well-built.

80. *an 't be*] if it be.

82. *privy maim*] hidden injury. (See next note.)

83. *standing upright*] with a sexual pun, continuing the joke of *skirmishing*
and *privy maim*.

crinkles] (a) bows; (b) shrinks, turns aside.

87. *very*] (a) truthful; (b) real.

some, and, by my troth, I think wholesome—and that's
news in a gallant of three and twenty. Liberal, that I
know; loving, that you know; and a man sure, else he
could never ha' purchased such a good name with   95
Hippolita the lusty widow in her husband's lifetime—an
'twere but for that report, sweetheart, would 'a were
thine! Commend a man for his qualities, but take a
husband as he is a plain-sufficient, naked man: such a one
is for your bed, and such a one is Signior Soranzo, my life 100
for 't.

Annabella. Sure the woman took her morning's draught too
soon.

Enter BERGETTO *and* POGGIO.

Putana. But look, sweetheart, look what thing comes now:
here's another of your ciphers to fill up the number. O,   105
brave old ape in a silken coat! Observe.

Bergetto. Didst thou think, Poggio, that I would spoil my new
clothes, and leave my dinner to fight?

Poggio. No, sir, I did not take you for so arrant a baby.

Bergetto. I am wiser than so; for I hope, Poggio, thou never 110
heard'st of an elder brother that was a coxcomb, didst,
Poggio?

Poggio. Never, indeed, sir, as long as they had either land or
money left them to inherit.

Bergetto. Is it possible, Poggio? O monstrous! Why, I'll under- 115

---

92. *wholesome*] free from venereal disease.

93. *Liberal*] generous (he has paid Putana to praise him).

96–7. *an 'twere but for*] if it were for nothing but.

97–8. *would 'a were thine*] would that he were yours. (Putana counts Soranzo's reputation as a lover of Hippolita as a point in his favour as a potential husband for Annabella.)

98. *qualities*] accomplishments.

99. *plain-sufficient*] sufficient in himself for ordinary needs.

102. *morning's draught*] morning drink of ale, wine or spirits. (Annabella implies, not very seriously, that Putana must be tipsy.)

105. *ciphers*] noughts.

106. *brave*] finely dressed.

ape . . . coat] unworthy person displaying wealth or finery.

111. *elder brother*] eldest son, in line to inherit the family fortune.

coxcomb] simpleton.

take, with a handful of silver, to buy a headful of wit at
any time. But sirrah, I have another purchase in hand: I
shall have the wench, mine uncle says. I will but wash my
face, and shift socks, and then have at her, i'faith!—Mark
my pace, Poggio.   [*Walks affectedly.*]   120
Poggio. Sir, I have seen an ass and a mule trot the Spanish
pavin with a better grace, I know not how often.
                              Exeunt [BERGETTO *and* POGGIO].
Annabella. This idiot haunts me too.
Putana. Ay, ay, he needs no description. The rich magnifico
that is below with your father, charge, Signior Donado   125
his uncle, for that he means to make this his cousin a
golden calf, thinks that you will be a right Israelite and fall
down to him presently; but I hope I have tutored you
better. They say a fool's bauble is a lady's playfellow; yet
you having wealth enough, you need not cast upon the   130
dearth of flesh, at any rate. Hang him, innocent!

                    Enter GIOVANNI.

Annabella. But see, Putana, see; what blessèd shape
          Of some celestial creature now appears?
          What man is he, that with such sad aspect
          Walks careless of himself?
Putana.   Where?
Annabella.   Look below.   135

---

117. *sirrah*] form of address used to command or rebuke, usually to men
or boys (but cf. II.vi.69).
119. *shift socks*] change my stockings.
have at her] I'll attack her.
119–20. *Mark my pace*] Watch how I walk.
122. *pavin*] pavane, a stately dance.
124. *magnifico*] grandee.
126. *for that*] because.
cousin] kinsman.
127. *golden calf*] i.e. wealthy simpleton.
right Israelite] like those who worshipped the golden calf in Exodus xxxii.
128. *presently*] immediately.
129. *fool's bauble*] stick with carved head carried by a professional jester.
(Often with bawdy suggestion, as here.)
130–1. *cast . . . flesh*] be influenced by the shortage of men.
131. *innocent*] simpleton, idiot.
134. *aspect*] look. (Stressed on second syllable.)

Putana. O, 'tis your brother, sweet—
Annabella.   Ha!
Putana.   'Tis your brother.
Annabella. Sure 'tis not he; this is some woeful thing
    Wrapped up in grief, some shadow of a man.
    Alas, he beats his breast, and wipes his eyes
    Drowned all in tears; methinks I hear him sigh.   140
    Let's down, Putana, and partake the cause;
    I know my brother, in the love he bears me,
    Will not deny me partage in his sadness.
    My soul is full of heaviness and fear.
                Exeunt [ANNABELLA *and* PUTANA].
Giovanni. Lost, I am lost; my fates have doomed my death;   145
    The more I strive, I love, the more I love,
    The less I hope; I see my ruin, certain.
    What judgement or endeavours could apply
    To my incurable and restless wounds
    I throughly have examined, but in vain.   150
    O that it were not in religion sin
    To make our love a god, and worship it!
    I have even wearied heaven with prayers, dried up
    The spring of my continual tears, even starved
    My veins with daily fasts; what wit or art   155
    Could counsel, I have practised. But alas,
    I find all these but dreams and old men's tales
    To fright unsteady youth; I'm still the same.
    Or I must speak, or burst; 'tis not, I know,
    My lust, but 'tis my fate that leads me on.   160
    Keep fear and low faint-hearted shame with slaves!
    I'll tell her that I love her, though my heart

---

141. *partake*] learn.

143. *partage in*] a share of.

144–5.] Nineteenth-century editors marked a change of scene to 'A Room in Florio's House'; but on the Elizabethan stage, with its absence of scenery, what had been a street scene could become delocalised.

150. *throughly*] thoroughly.

155. *art*] medical lore.

159. *Or*] either.

161.] 'Let fear and cowardly shame dwell with ignoble wretches!'

162–3. *though . . . attempt*] though the attempt cost me my heart, i.e. my life.

Were rated at the price of that attempt.
O me! She comes.

Enter ANNABELLA *and* PUTANA.

Annabella.   Brother!
Giovanni. [*Aside*]   If such a thing
     As courage dwell in men, ye heavenly powers,   165
     Now double all that virtue in my tongue.
Annabella. Why brother, will you not speak to me?
Giovanni. Yes; how d'ee, sister?
Annabella.   Howsoever I am,
     Methinks you are not well.
Putana. Bless us, why are you so sad, sir?   170
Giovanni. Let me entreat you leave us awhile, Putana,—
     Sister, I would be private with you.
Annabella. Withdraw, Putana.
Putana. I will. [*Aside*] If this were any other company for her,
     I should think my absence an office of some credit; but   175
     I will leave them together.   *Exit.*
Giovanni. Come, sister, lend your hand, let's walk together.
     I hope you need not blush to walk with me;
     Here's none but you and I.
Annabella. How's this?   180
Giovanni. Faith, I mean no harm.
Annabella. Harm?
Giovanni. No, good faith; how is 't with 'ee?
Annabella. [*Aside*] I trust he be not frantic. [*To him*] I am very
     well, brother.   185
Giovanni. Trust me, but I am sick; I fear so sick
     'Twill cost my life.
Annabella. Mercy forbid it! 'Tis not so, I hope.
Giovanni. I think you love me, sister.
Annabella. Yes, you know I do.   190
Giovanni. I know 't, indeed.—Y' are very fair.
Annabella. Nay, then I see you have a merry sickness.
Giovanni. That's as it proves. The poets feign, I read,

---

175. *office . . . credit*] good turn deserving a reward, i.e. for letting a man
have access to Annabella.
     184. *frantic*] mad.
     193. *proves*] turns out.

That Juno for her forehead did exceed
All other goddesses; but I durst swear   195
Your forehead exceeds hers, as hers did theirs.
Annabella. Troth, this is pretty!
Giovanni.   Such a pair of stars
As are thine eyes would, like Promethean fire,
If gently glanced, give life to senseless stones.
Annabella. Fie upon 'ee!   200
Giovanni. The lily and the rose, most sweetly strange,
Upon your dimpled cheeks do strive for change.
Such lips would tempt a saint; such hands as those
Would make an anchorite lascivious.
Annabella. D'ee mock me, or flatter me?   205
Giovanni. If you would see a beauty more exact
Than art can counterfeit or nature frame,
Look in your glass, and there behold your own.
Annabella. O, you are a trim youth.
Giovanni. Here!   *Offers his dagger to her.*
Annabella.   What to do?
Giovanni.   And here's my breast, strike home!   210
Rip up my bosom, there thou shalt behold
A heart in which is writ the truth I speak.
Why stand 'ee?
Annabella.   Are you earnest?
Giovanni.   Yes, most earnest;
You cannot love—
Annabella.   Whom?
Giovanni.   Me. My tortured soul
Hath felt affliction in the heat of death.   215
O Annabella, I am quite undone:
The love of thee, my sister, and the view
Of thy immortal beauty hath untuned

---

194. *Juno*] queen of the Roman gods, Jupiter's sister and wife.
198. *Promethean fire*] fire stolen from heaven by Prometheus, who used it
to give life to men and women he had made from clay.
201. *strange*] intense.
202. *change*] interchange.
204. *anchorite*] religious recluse, hermit.
209. *trim*] fine, nice.
213. *stand 'ee*] do you hesitate.
215. *affliction . . . death*] suffering intense enough to be fatal.

All harmony both of my rest and life.
Why d'ee not strike?
Annabella.   Forbid it, my just fears!   220
    If this be true, 'twere fitter I were dead.
Giovanni. True, Annabella? 'Tis no time to jest.
    I have too long suppressed the hidden flames
    That almost have consumed me; I have spent
    Many a silent night in sighs and groans,   225
    Ran over all my thoughts, despised my fate,
    Reasoned against the reasons of my love,
    Done all that smoothed-cheek Virtue could advise,
    But found all bootless. 'Tis my destiny
    That you must either love, or I must die.   230
Annabella. Comes this in sadness from you?
Giovanni.   Let some mischief
    Befall me soon, if I dissemble aught.
Annabella. You are my brother, Giovanni.
Giovanni.   You
    My sister, Annabella; I know this;
    And could afford you instance why to love   235
    So much the more for this; to which intent
    Wise Nature first in your creation meant
    To make you mine; else 't had been sin and foul
    To share one beauty to a double soul.
    Nearness in birth or blood doth but persuade   240
    A nearer nearness in affection.
    I have asked counsel of the holy Church,
    Who tells me I may love you, and 'tis just
    That since I may, I should; and will, yes, will!

---

226. *despised my fate*] defied my destiny.

228. *smoothed-cheek*] smooth-cheeked. Virtue is personified as either a beardless youth or a smug, well-groomed counsellor.

229. *bootless*] useless.

231. *sadness*] seriousness.

232. *dissemble*] pretend.

235. *afford you instance*] show you reason.

239.] In Neoplatonic theory, true love arose from an affinity between 'twin souls', which should reveal itself in physical likeness.

240. *persuade*] argue for, recommend.

    Must I now live, or die?

Annabella.   Live. Thou hast won   245

    The field, and never fought; what thou hast urged,

    My captive heart had long ago resolved.

    I blush to tell thee—but I'll tell thee now—

    For every sigh that thou hast spent for me,

    I have sighed ten; for every tear shed twenty;   250

    And not so much for that I loved, as that

    I durst not say I loved; nor scarcely think it.

Giovanni. Let not this music be a dream, ye gods,

    For pity's sake I beg 'ee!

Annabella.   On my knees,   *She kneels.*

    Brother, even by our mother's dust, I charge you,   255

    Do not betray me to your mirth or hate.

    Love me, or kill me, brother.

Giovanni.   On my knees,   *He kneels.*

    Sister, even by my mother's dust I charge you,

    Do not betray me to your mirth or hate.

    Love me, or kill me, sister.   260

Annabella. You mean good sooth, then?

Giovanni.   In good troth I do,

    And so do you, I hope. Say, I'm in earnest.

Annabella. I'll swear 't, and I.

Giovanni.   And I, and by this kiss—

                       Kisses her.

    Once more; yet once more; now let's rise—by this,

    I would not change this minute for Elysium.   265

    What must we now do?

Annabella.   What you will.

Giovanni.   Come then;

    After so many tears as we have wept,

    Let's learn to court in smiles, to kiss and sleep.

                       Exeunt.

---

251. *for that*] because.

261. *mean good sooth*] are really speaking the truth.

262. *Say . . . earnest*] i.e. 'I'm serious about this, tell me you are too.'

265. *Elysium*] in classical mythology, the happy dwelling-place of blest souls.

[I. iii]

Enter FLORIO *and* DONADO.

Florio. Signior Donado, you have said enough.
    I understand you, but would have you know
    I will not force my daughter 'gainst her will.
    You see I have but two, a son and her;
    And he is so devoted to his book,   5
    As I must tell you true, I doubt his health.
    Should he miscarry, all my hopes rely
    Upon my girl. As for worldly fortune,
    I am, I thank my stars, blessed with enough;
    My care is how to match her to her liking;   10
    I would not have her marry wealth, but love,
    And if she like your nephew, let him have her.
    Here's all that I can say.
Donado.   Sir, you say well,
    Like a true father, and for my part, I,
    If the young folks can like—'twixt you and me—   15
    Will promise to assure my nephew presently
    Three thousand florins yearly during life,
    And, after I am dead, my whole estate.
Florio. 'Tis a fair proffer, sir; meantime your nephew
    Shall have free passage to commence his suit.   20
    If he can thrive, he shall have my consent.
    So for this time I'll leave you, signior.   *Exit.*
Donado.   Well,
    Here's hope yet, if my nephew would have wit;
    But he is such another dunce, I fear
    He'll never win the wench. When I was young   25
    I could have done 't, i'faith, and so shall he
    If he will learn of me; and in good time
    He comes himself.

Enter BERGETTO *and* POGGIO.

I.iii.6. *doubt*] fear for.
7. *miscarry*] come to harm.
8. *girl*] a disyllable in Ford ('girrel'); cf. II.i.79.
24. *such another dunce*] such a perfect dunce.
27. *in good time*] just at the right moment.

How now, Bergetto, whither away so fast?

Bergetto. O uncle, I have heard the strangest news that ever 30
came out of the mint—have I not, Poggio?

Poggio. Yes indeed, sir.

Donado. What news, Bergetto?

Bergetto. Why, look ye, uncle, my barber told me just now
that there is a fellow come to town who undertakes to 35
make a mill go without the mortal help of any water or
wind, only with sandbags! And this fellow hath a strange
horse, a most excellent beast I'll assure you, uncle, my
barber says, whose head, to the wonder of all Christian
people, stands just behind where his tail is—is 't not true, 40
Poggio?

Poggio. So the barber swore, forsooth.

Donado. And you are running thither?

Bergetto. Ay, forsooth, uncle.

Donado. Wilt thou be a fool still? Come, sir, you shall not go; 45
you have more mind of a puppet-play than on the business I told ye. Why, thou great baby, wou't never have
wit? Wou't make thyself a May-game to all the world?

Poggio. [*To Bergetto*] Answer for yourself, master.

Bergetto. Why uncle, should I sit at home still, and not go 50
abroad to see fashions like other gallants?

Donado. To see hobby-horses! What wise talk, I pray, had you
with Annabella, when you were at Signior Florio's house?

Bergetto. O, the wench. Ud's sa' me, uncle, I tickled her with
a rare speech, that I made her almost burst her belly with 55
laughing.

Donado. Nay, I think so, and what speech was 't?

---

34. *barber*] a traditional source of news and gossip.

37. *only with sandbags*] apparently a device alleged to produce perpetual
motion.

37–40. *a strange horse . . . tail is*] Customers who paid to see 'the horse with
the head where its tail ought to be' would find its tail tied to the manger.

48. *May-game*] i.e. laughing-stock.

51. *see fashions*] see life, see what's going on.

52. *hobby-horses*] performers costumed as horses in the morris dance (a
folk custom) and other 'May-games'.

54. *Ud's sa' me*] God save me.

55. *rare*] excellent.

Bergetto. What did I say, Poggio?

Poggio. Forsooth, my master said that he loved her almost as
    well as he loved parmasent, and swore—I'll be sworn for   60
    him—that she wanted but such a nose as his was to be as
    pretty a young woman as any was in Parma.

Donado. O, gross!

Bergetto. Nay, uncle, then she asked me whether my father
    had any more children than myself; and I said, 'No,   65
    'twere better he should have had his brains knocked out
    first'.

Donado. This is intolerable.

Bergetto. Then said she, 'Will Signior Donado your uncle
    leave you all his wealth?'   70

Donado. Ha! That was good. Did she harp upon that string?

Bergetto. Did she harp upon that string? Ay, that she did. I
    answered, 'Leave me all his wealth? Why, woman, he
    hath no other wit; if he had, he should hear on 't to his
    everlasting glory and confusion. I know,' quoth I, 'I am   75
    his white boy, and will not be gulled'; and with that she
    fell into a great smile, and went away. Nay, I did fit her.

Donado. Ah, sirrah, then I see there is no changing of nature.
    Well, Bergetto, I fear thou wilt be a very ass still.

Bergetto. I should be sorry for that, uncle.   80

Donado. Come, come you home with me. Since you are no
    better a speaker, I'll have you write to her after some
    courtly manner, and enclose some rich jewel in the letter.

Bergetto. Ay, marry, that will be excellent.

Donado. Peace, innocent!   85
    Once in my time I'll set my wits to school;
    If all fail, 'tis but the fortune of a fool.

Bergetto. Poggio, 'twill do, Poggio!   *Exeunt.*

---

    60. *parmasent*] Parmesan cheese.
    61. *wanted*] needed, lacked.
    74. *wit*] thought.
    75. *confusion*] damnation, destruction.
    76. *white boy*] favourite (literally, fair-haired boy).
    gulled] cheated.
    77. *fit*] fitly answer, cope with.

Act II

Enter GIOVANNI *and* ANNABELLA, *as from their chamber.*

Giovanni. Come, Annabella, no more sister now
   But love, a name more gracious. Do not blush,
   Beauty's sweet wonder, but be proud, to know
   That yielding thou hast conquered, and inflamed
   A heart whose tribute is thy brother's life.   5
Annabella. And mine is his. O, how these stol'n contents
   Would print a modest crimson on my cheeks,
   Had any but my heart's delight prevailed!
Giovanni. I marvel why the chaster of your sex
   Should think this pretty toy called maidenhead   10
   So strange a loss, when being lost, 'tis nothing,
   And you are still the same.
Annabella.   'Tis well for you;
   Now you can talk.
Giovanni.   Music as well consists
   In th' ear as in the playing.
Annabella.   O, y' are wanton!
   Tell on 't, y' are best, do.
Giovanni.   Thou wilt chide me, then?   15
   Kiss me, so. [*They kiss.*] Thus hung Jove on Leda's neck

II.i.o.S.D. *as from their chamber*] apparently indicating an entrance in the
gallery above.

5.] probably 'The tribute paid by my heart is the offer of my whole life',
though Ford sometimes uses *life* to mean 'bliss, heaven' (II.ii.11).

6. *contents*] pleasures. (Accented on second syllable.)

11. *strange*] important.

12. *well for you*] all right for you.

13–14. *Music . . . playing*] a metaphor: 'The more passive partner enjoys
sex as well as the active.'

14. *wanton*] naughty.

16. *on Leda's neck*] Jupiter took refuge in Leda's bosom in the form of a
swan, and so seduced her.

And sucked divine ambrosia from her lips.
I envy not the mightiest man alive,
But hold myself in being king of thee
More great than were I king of all the world.   20
But I shall lose you, sweetheart.
Annabella.   But you shall not.
Giovanni. You must be married, mistress.
Annabella.   Yes, to whom?
Giovanni. Someone must have you.
Annabella.   You must.
Giovanni.   Nay, some other.
Annabella. Now prithee do not speak so without jesting.
    You'll make me weep in earnest.
Giovanni.   What, you will not!   25
    But tell me, sweet, canst thou be dared to swear
    That thou wilt live to me, and to no other?
Annabella. By both our loves I dare; for, didst thou know,
    My Giovanni, how all suitors seem
    To my eyes hateful, thou wouldst trust me then.   30
Giovanni. Enough, I take thy word. Sweet, we must part.
    Remember what thou vow'st; keep well my heart.
Annabella. Will you be gone?
Giovanni. I must.
Annabella. When to return?   35
Giovanni. Soon.
Annabella. Look you do.
Giovanni. Farewell.   *Exit.*
Annabella. Go where thou wilt, in mind I'll keep thee here,
    And where thou art, I know I shall be there.—   40
    Guardian!

Enter PUTANA.

Putana. Child, how is 't, child? Well, thank heaven, ha?
Annabella. O guardian, what a paradise of joy
    Have I passed over!

---

17. *ambrosia*] the sweet, scented food of the gods, which conferred immortality.
    23. *have you*] a sexual pun.
    26. *be dared*] be bold enough.
    37. *Look you do*] Mind you do.

Putana. Nay, what a paradise of joy have you passed under!   45
  Why, now I commend thee, charge; fear nothing, sweet-
  heart. What though he be your brother? Your brother's a
  man, I hope, and I say still, if a young wench feel the fit
  upon her, let her take anybody, father or brother, all is
  one.   50
Annabella. I would not have it known for all the world.
Putana. Nor I indeed, for the speech of the people; else 'twere
  nothing.
Florio. (*Within*) Daughter Annabella!
Annabella. O me, my father!—Here, sir!—Reach my work.   55
Florio. (*Within*) What are you doing?
Annabella.   So, let him come now.

   Enter FLORIO, RICHARDETTO *like a Doctor of Physic,*
    and PHILOTIS *with a lute in her hand.*

Florio. So hard at work; that's well! You lose no time.
  Look, I have brought you company: here's one,
  A learned doctor, lately come from Padua,
  Much skilled in physic; and for that I see   60
  You have of late been sickly, I entreated
  This reverend man to visit you some time.
Annabella. [*To Richardetto*] Y' are very welcome, sir.
Richardetto.   I thank you, mistress.
  Loud fame in large report hath spoke your praise
  As well for virtue as perfection;   65
  For which I have been bold to bring with me
  A kinswoman of mine, a maid, for song

---

 45. *passed under*] Putana picks up Annabella's *passed over* ('passed
through') to make a crude joke.

 48. *fit*] impulse, mood.

 49–50. *all is one*] it makes no difference.

 52. *for*] because of.

 55. *Reach my work*] Hand me my needlework; a visual irony, as the
virtuous woman was traditionally represented as so employed.

 56.1.S.D. Physic] medicine.

 59. *Padua*] a city famous for its university.

 60. *for that*] since.

 62. *reverend*] worthy of respect.

 64. *large*] full and free.

 65. *perfection*] of beauty or accomplishments.

And music, one perhaps will give content.
Please you to know her?
Annabella.   They are parts I love,
And she for them most welcome.
Philotis.   Thank you, lady.   70
Florio. Sir, now you know my house, pray make not strange;
And if you find my daughter need your art,
I'll be your paymaster.
Richardetto.   Sir, what I am
She shall command.
Florio.   You shall bind me to you.—
Daughter, I must have conference with you   75
About some matters that concerns us both.—
Good master doctor, please you but walk in,
We'll crave a little of your cousin's cunning.
I think my girl hath not quite forgot
To touch an instrument; she could have done 't;   80
We'll hear them both.
Richardetto.   I'll wait upon you, sir.   *Exeunt.*

[II. ii]

Enter SORANZO *in his study, reading a book.*

Soranzo. 'Love's measure is extreme, the comfort pain,
The life unrest, and the reward disdain.'
What's here? Look 't o'er again. 'Tis so, so writes

---

69. *parts*] talents (but with a hidden suggestion also of 'sexual organs'; an echo of Annabella's initiation, like other words in this conversation).

71. *make not strange*] don't stand on ceremony.

74. *bind me to you*] i.e. bind me by ties of gratitude.

78. *cunning*] skill.

79. *girl*] a disyllable, as at I.iii.8.

80. *touch*] (a) play; (b) handle, excite.

instrument] with the extra, unintended meaning of 'penis'.

she . . . done 't] she was able to do it, could play (again, with an unintended sexual meaning).

II.ii.0.1.S.D. *in his study*] Soranzo is seemingly disclosed within a 'discovery space' backstage. Probably he comes forward at 25, if not earlier.

1. *measure*] balance, moderation, the opposite of 'extreme'; the first of four paradoxes typical of Petrarchan love poetry.

This smooth licentious poet in his rhymes.
But Sannazar, thou liest, for had thy bosom   5
Felt such oppression as is laid on mine,
Thou wouldst have kissed the rod that made the smart.
To work, then, happy Muse, and contradict
What Sannazar hath in his envy writ: [*Writes.*]
'Love's measure is the mean, sweet his annoys,   10
His pleasures life, and his reward all joys.'
Had Annabella lived when Sannazar
Did in his brief encomium celebrate
Venice, that queen of cities, he had left
That verse which gained him such a sum of gold,   15
And for one only look from Annabell
Had writ of her, and her diviner cheeks.
O, how my thoughts are—

Vasques. (*Within*) Pray forbear, in rules of civility; let me give
notice on 't. I shall be taxed of my neglect of duty and   20
service.

Soranzo. What rude intrusion interrupts my peace?
Can I be nowhere private?

Vasques. (*Within*) Troth, you wrong your modesty.

Soranzo. What's the matter, Vasques, who is 't?   25

Enter HIPPOLITA *and* VASQUES.

Hippolita. 'Tis I.
Do you know me now? Look, perjured man, on her
Whom thou and thy distracted lust have wronged.

---

4. *licentious*] (a) erotic; (b) taking liberties with the language.

his rhymes] perhaps Sannazaro's *Rime* (1540), though these lines have not been found.

5. *Sannazar*] Jacopo Sannazaro (1455–1530), Neapolitan pastoral poet, best known for his *Arcadia* (1501–4).

7. *kissed the rod*] accepted the punishment gladly.

10. *Love's . . . mean*] Love's standard is the true one.

11. *life*] bliss, heaven.

13. *encomium*] eulogy; Sannazaro's six lines of Latin verse in praise of Venice earned him 600 crowns.

14. *had left*] would have abandoned.

20. *taxed of*] blamed for.

28. *distracted*] drawn first in one direction, then in another.

Thy sensual rage of blood hath made my youth
A scorn to men and angels; and shall I   30
Be now a foil to thy unsated change?
Thou know'st, false wanton, when my modest fame
Stood free from stain or scandal, all the charms
Of hell or sorcery could not prevail
Against the honour of my chaster bosom.   35
Thine eyes did plead in tears, thy tongue in oaths
Such and so many, that a heart of steel
Would have been wrought to pity, as was mine.
And shall the conquest of my lawful bed,
My husband's death urged on by his disgrace,   40
My loss of womanhood, be ill rewarded
With hatred and contempt? No, know, Soranzo,
I have a spirit doth as much distaste
The slavery of fearing thee as thou
Dost loathe the memory of what hath passed.   45
Soranzo. Nay, dear Hippolita—
Hippolita.   Call me not dear,
Nor think with supple words to smooth the grossness
Of my abuses. 'Tis not your new mistress,
Your goodly Madam Merchant, shall triumph
On my dejection. Tell her thus from me,   50
My birth was nobler, and by much more free.
Soranzo. You are too violent.
Hippolita.   You are too double
In your dissimulation. Seest thou this,
This habit, these black mourning weeds of care?
'Tis thou art cause of this, and hast divorced   55
My husband from his life and me from him,

---

29. *sensual rage of blood*] violence of sexual passion.

31. *foil*] contrast, to heighten enjoyment elsewhere.

32. *wanton*] irresponsible seeker after pleasure.

40. *urged on*] hastened.

41. *womanhood*] status as an honourable woman.

43. *doth . . . distaste*] that as much dislikes.

49. *Madam Merchant*] Annabella, whose father's wealth has been gained by trade.

triumph] stressed on the second syllable, as at IV.iii.64.

50. *dejection*] downfall.

51. *free*] honourable.

And made me widow in my widowhood.

Soranzo. Will you yet hear?

Hippolita.   More of thy perjuries?
    Thy soul is drowned too deeply in those sins;
    Thou need'st not add to th' number.

Soranzo.   Then I'll leave you;   60
    You are past all rules of sense.

Hippolita.   And thou of grace.

Vasques. Fie, mistress, you are not near the limits of reason. If
    my lord had a resolution as noble as virtue itself, you take
    the course to unedge it all.—Sir, I beseech you do not
    perplex her; griefs, alas, will have a vent. I dare undertake   65
    Madam Hippolita will now freely hear you.

Soranzo. Talk to a woman frantic! Are these the fruits of your
    love?

Hippolita. They are the fruits of thy untruth, false man!
    Didst thou not swear, whilst yet my husband lived,   70
    That thou wouldst wish no happiness on earth
    More than to call me wife? Didst thou not vow
    When he should die to marry me? For which
    The devil in my blood, and thy protests,
    Caused me to counsel him to undertake   75
    A voyage to Ligorne—for that we heard
    His brother there was dead, and left a daughter
    Young and unfriended, who with much ado
    I wished him to bring hither. He did so,
    And went; and, as thou know'st, died on the way.   80
    Unhappy man, to buy his death so dear

---

57. *made . . . widowhood*] either (a) by estranging me from my husband
before he died; or (b) by deserting me after his death.

61.] Soranzo tells Hippolita that she is beyond reason; she replies that he
is beyond even grace, i.e. God's forgiveness, held to reach farther than
reason.

62. *not . . . reason*] quite unreasonable.

63. *resolution*] firm purpose; Vasques hints that Soranzo had intended
reparation.

64. *unedge*] blunt, discourage.

74. *protests*] protestations, promises (stressed on the second syllable).

76. *voyage*] here a land journey.

Ligorne] Livorno, a large seaport less than 100 miles from Parma, reached
by crossing dangerous mountain districts.

With my advice! Yet thou for whom I did it
Forget'st thy vows, and leav'st me to my shame.
Soranzo. Who could help this?
Hippolita.   Who? Perjured man, thou couldst,
If thou hadst faith or love.
Soranzo.   You are deceived.   85
The vows I made, if you remember well,
Were wicked and unlawful; 'twere more sin
To keep them than to break them. As for me,
I cannot mask my penitence. Think thou
How much thou hast digressed from honest shame   90
In bringing of a gentleman to death
Who was thy husband—such a one as he,
So noble in his quality, condition,
Learning, behaviour, entertainment, love,
As Parma could not show a braver man.   95
Vasques. You do not well; this was not your promise.
Soranzo. I care not; let her know her monstrous life.
Ere I'll be servile to so black a sin
I'll be a corse.—Woman, come here no more.
Learn to repent and die, for, by my honour,   100
I hate thee and thy lust. You have been too foul.
                                        [*Exit.*]
Vasques. This part has been scurvily played.
Hippolita. How foolishly this beast contemns his fate,
And shuns the use of that which I more scorn
Than I once loved, his love! But let him go.   105

---

89. *mask my penitence*] hide the fact that I now repent (i.e. of our affair and
its consequences).

90. *digressed from honest shame*] deviated from honour and modesty.

93. *quality*] rank.
condition] wealth and social status.

94. *entertainment*] hospitality.

95. *braver*] finer.

96.] Vasques again tries to make Hippolita believe that Soranzo had
meant to make reparation (cf. 63 above), but from now on he also pretends
to blame Soranzo in order to gain Hippolita's confidence.

99. *a corse*] a corpse; though possibly Ford wrote 'accurst'.

102. *scurvily played*] badly acted.

103. *contemns his fate*] disregards his approaching doom.

My vengeance shall give comfort to his woe.

She offers to go away.

Vasques. Mistress, mistress, Madam Hippolita; pray, a word
    or two.

Hippolita. With me, sir?

Vasques. With you, if you please.   110

Hippolita. What is 't?

Vasques. I know you are infinitely moved now, and you think
    you have cause; some I confess you have, but sure not so
    much as you imagine.

Hippolita. Indeed!   115

Vasques. O you were miserably bitter, which you followed
    even to the last syllable; faith, you were somewhat too
    shrewd. By my life, you could not have took my lord in a
    worse time since I first knew him; tomorrow you shall
    find him a new man.   120

Hippolita. Well, I shall wait his leisure.

Vasques. Fie, this is not a hearty patience, it comes sourly
    from you; troth, let me persuade you for once.

Hippolita. [*Aside*] I have it, and it shall be so; thanks, oppor-
    tunity! [*To him*] Persuade me to what?   125

Vasques. Visit him in some milder temper. O, if you could but
    master a little your female spleen, how might you win
    him!

Hippolita. He will never love me. Vasques, thou hast been a
    too trusty servant to such a master, and I believe thy   130
    reward in the end will fall out like mine.

Vasques. So perhaps too.

Hippolita. Resolve thyself it will. Had I one so true, so truly
    honest, so secret to my counsels as thou hast been to him
    and his, I should think it a slight acquittance not only to   135
    make him master of all I have, but even of myself.

Vasques. O, you are a noble gentlewoman!

---

106. *his woe*] the woe he has caused.
116. *followed*] kept up.
118. *shrewd*] shrewish, abusive.
131. *fall out*] turn out.
133. *Resolve thyself*] make up your mind that.
135. *acquittance*] discharge of debt; reward.

Hippolita. Wou't thou feed always upon hopes? Well, I know
    thou art wise, and seest the reward of an old servant daily
    what it is.   140
Vasques. Beggary and neglect.
Hippolita. True; but Vasques, wert thou mine, and wouldst
    be private to me and my designs, I here protest myself,
    and all what I can else call mine, should be at thy dispose.
Vasques. [*Aside*] Work you that way, old mole? Then I have   145
    the wind of you. [*To her*] I were not worthy of it, by any
    desert that could lie within my compass; if I could—
Hippolita. What then?
Vasques. I should then hope to live in these my old years with
    rest and security.   150
Hippolita. Give me thy hand. Now promise but thy silence,
    And help to bring to pass a plot I have.
    And here in sight of heaven, that being done,
    I make thee lord of me and mine estate.
Vasques. Come, you are merry. This is such a happiness that   155
    I can neither think or believe.
Hippolita. Promise thy secrecy, and 'tis confirmed.
Vasques. Then here I call our good genii for witnesses, what-
    soever your designs are, or against whomsoever, I will not
    only be a special actor therein, but never disclose it till it   160
    be effected.
Hippolita. I take thy word, and with that, thee for mine.
    Come then, let's more confer of this anon.
    On this delicious bane my thoughts shall banquet:
    Revenge shall sweeten what my griefs have tasted.   165
                             Exeunt.

---

143. *protest*] declare.
145–6. *have . . . you*] guess your intention. (A hunter can locate the quarry
when the wind brings its scent to him.)
155. *happiness*] good fortune.
158. *good genii*] in classical mythology, protective spirits, 'guardian
angels'.
163. *anon*] straight away.
164. *bane*] poison. (Hippolita may speak this last couplet to herself, or to
the audience.)

[II. iii]

> *Enter* RICHARDETTO [*disguised still as a physician*]
> *and* PHILOTIS.

Richardetto. Thou seest, my lovely niece, these strange
  mishaps,
 How all my fortunes turn to my disgrace,
 Wherein I am but as a looker-on,
 Whiles others act my shame, and I am silent.
Philotis. But uncle, wherein can this borrowed shape   5
 Give you content?
Richardetto.   I'll tell thee, gentle niece:
 Thy wanton aunt in her lascivious riots
 Lives now secure, thinks I am surely dead
 In my late journey to Ligorne for you—
 As I have caused it to be rumoured out.   10
 Now would I see with what an impudence
 She gives scope to her loose adultery,
 And how the common voice allows hereof;
 Thus far I have prevailed.
Philotis.   Alas, I fear
 You mean some strange revenge.
Richardetto.   O, be not troubled; 15
 Your ignorance shall plead for you in all.
 But to our business: what, you learnt for certain
 How Signior Florio means to give his daughter
 In marriage to Soranzo?
Philotis.   Yes, for certain.
Richardetto. But how find you young Annabella's love 20
 Inclined to him?
Philotis.   For aught I could perceive,
 She neither fancies him or any else.

 II.iii.5. *borrowed shape*] disguise (as a physician).
 7. *lascivious riots*] sensual indulgences.
 8. *secure*] relaxed, unsuspecting.
 13. *the common voice allows*] public opinion judges.
 16.] i.e. 'Since you are ignorant of my plans, you will not be blamed for
them.'

Richardetto. There's mystery in that which time must show.
    She used you kindly?
Philotis.   Yes.
Richardetto.   And craved your company?
Philotis. Often.
Richardetto.   'Tis well, it goes as I could wish.   25
    I am the doctor now, and as for you,
    None knows you; if all fail not we shall thrive.
    But who comes here?

                    Enter GRIMALDI.

                    I know him, 'tis Grimaldi:
    A Roman and a soldier, near allied
    Unto the Duke of Montferrato; one   30
    Attending on the nuncio of the Pope
    That now resides in Parma, by which means
    He hopes to get the love of Annabella.
Grimaldi. Save you, sir.
Richardetto.   And you, sir.
Grimaldi.   I have heard
    Of your approvèd skill, which through the city   35
    Is freely talked of, and would crave your aid.
Richardetto. For what, sir?
Grimaldi.   Marry sir, for this—
    But I would speak in private.
Richardetto.   Leave us, cousin.
                              Exit PHILOTIS.
Grimaldi. I love fair Annabella, and would know
    Whether in arts there may not be receipts   40
    To move affection.
Richardetto.   Sir, perhaps there may,
    But these will nothing profit you.
Grimaldi.   Not me?
Richardetto. Unless I be mistook, you are a man
    Greatly in favour with the Cardinal.

---

    31. *nuncio of the Pope*] papal representative.
    34. *Save you*] God save you.
    38. *cousin*] i.e. niece.
    40. *arts*] medicine.
    40–1. *receipts . . . affection*] recipes to arouse love.
    42. *nothing*] not at all.

Grimaldi. What of that?

Richardetto.   In duty to his grace,   45
    I will be bold to tell you, if you seek
    To marry Florio's daughter, you must first
    Remove a bar 'twixt you and her.

Grimaldi.   Who's that?

Richardetto. Soranzo is the man that hath her heart,
    And while he lives be sure you cannot speed.   50

Grimaldi. Soranzo—what, mine enemy, is 't he?

Richardetto. Is he your enemy?

Grimaldi. The man I hate worse than confusion!
    I'll kill him straight.

Richardetto.   Nay, then take mine advice,
    Even for his grace's sake the Cardinal: 55
    I'll find a time when he and she do meet,
    Of which I'll give you notice, and, to be sure
    He shall not 'scape you, I'll provide a poison
    To dip your rapier's point in. If he had
    As many heads as Hydra had, he dies.   60

Grimaldi. But shall I trust thee, doctor?

Richardetto.   As yourself;
    Doubt not in aught. [*Aside*] Thus shall the fates decree:
    By me Soranzo falls that ruined me.   *Exeunt.*

[II. iv]

Enter DONADO, BERGETTO *and* POGGIO.

Donado. Well, sir, I must be content to be both your secretary
    and your messenger myself. I cannot tell what this letter
    may work, but, as sure as I am alive, if thou come once to
    talk with her, I fear thou wou't mar whatsoever I make.

Bergetto. You make, uncle? Why, am not I big enough to carry   5
    mine own letter, I pray?

Donado. Ay, ay, carry a fool's head o' thy own. Why, thou
    dunce, wouldst thou write a letter, and carry it thyself?

---

50. *speed*] succeed.

53. *confusion*] damnation.

54. *straight*] straight away.

60. *Hydra*] in classical mythology, a monster with many heads; if one was
cut off, two grew in its place.

Bergetto. Yes, that I would, and read it to her with my own
　　mouth; for you must think, if she will not believe me   10
　　myself when she hears me speak, she will not believe
　　another's handwriting. O, you think I am a blockhead,
　　uncle! No, sir, Poggio knows I have indited a letter my-
　　self, so I have.

Poggio. Yes truly, sir, I have it in my pocket.   15

Donado. A sweet one no doubt. Pray let's see 't.

Bergetto. I cannot read my own hand very well, Poggio; read
　　it, Poggio.

Donado. Begin.

Poggio. (*Reads*) 'Most dainty and honey-sweet mistress, I   20
　　could call you fair, and lie as fast as any that loves you,
　　but my uncle being the elder man I leave it to him, as
　　more fit for his age and the colour of his beard. I am wise
　　enough to tell you I can board where I see occasion, or,
　　if you like my uncle's wit better than mine, you shall   25
　　marry me; if you like mine better than his, I will marry
　　you in spite of your teeth. So, commending my best parts
　　to you, I rest

　　　　Yours upwards and downwards, or you may choose,
　　　　　　　　　　　　Bergetto.'   30

Bergetto. Ah, ha! Here's stuff, uncle!

Donado. Here's stuff indeed to shame us all. Pray, whose
　　advice did you take in this learned letter?

Poggio. None, upon my word, but mine own.

Bergetto. And mine, uncle, believe it, nobody's else; 'twas   35
　　mine own brain, I thank a good wit for 't.

Donado. Get you home, sir, and look you keep within doors
　　till I return.

Bergetto. How! That were a jest indeed. I scorn it, i'faith.

Donado. What, you do not!   40

Bergetto. Judge me, but I do now.

Poggio. Indeed sir, 'tis very unhealthy.

Donado. Well, sir, if I hear any of your apish running to

II.iv.13. *indited*] composed.
24. *board*] engage closely (in conversation or embraces).
occasion] a good opportunity.
27. *your teeth*] your opposition.

    motions and fopperies till I come back, you were as good
    no. Look to 't.   *Exit.*   45
Bergetto. Poggio, shall 's steal to see this horse with the head
    in 's tail?
Poggio. Ay, but you must take heed of whipping.
Bergetto. Dost take me for a child, Poggio? Come, honest
    Poggio.   50
                                          Exeunt.

[II. v]

                Enter Friar *and* GIOVANNI.

Friar. Peace! Thou hast told a tale whose every word
    Threatens eternal slaughter to the soul.
    I'm sorry I have heard it; would mine ears
    Had been one minute deaf, before the hour
    That thou cam'st to me! O young man cast away,   5
    By the religious number of mine order,
    I day and night have waked my agèd eyes,
    Above my strength, to weep on thy behalf.
    But heaven is angry, and, be thou resolved,
    Thou art a man remarked to taste a mischief.   10
    Look for 't; though it come late, it will come sure.
Giovanni. Father, in this you are uncharitable.
    What I have done, I'll prove both fit and good.
    It is a principle, which you have taught
    When I was yet your scholar, that the frame   15

---

44. *motions*] puppet shows.
fopperies] follies.
44–5. *you were as good no*] you'll regret it.
46. *shall 's*] shall we.

II.v.5. *cast away*] lost, damned.
6. *number*] company (of his order of friars).
9. *resolved*] assured.
10. *remarked*] marked out.
mischief] misfortune.
14–26.] These lines are the stage equivalent of a specious argument in syllogisms (units of formal logic), appropriate to a young student when logic was a part of the university curriculum.

And composition of the mind doth follow
The frame and composition of body;
So where the body's furniture is beauty,
The mind's must needs be virtue; which allowed,
Virtue itself is reason but refined,   20
And love the quintessence of that. This proves
My sister's beauty, being rarely fair,
Is rarely virtuous; chiefly in her love,
And chiefly in that love, her love to me.
If hers to me, then so is mine to her;   25
Since in like causes are effects alike.

Friar. O ignorance in knowledge! Long ago,
How often have I warned thee this before!
Indeed, if we were sure there were no deity,
Nor heaven nor hell, then to be led alone   30
By nature's light—as were philosophers
Of elder times—might instance some defence.
But 'tis not so. Then, madman, thou wilt find
That nature is in heaven's positions blind.

Giovanni. Your age o'errules you; had you youth like mine,   35
You'd make her love your heaven, and her divine.

Friar. Nay, then I see th' art too far sold to hell;
It lies not in the compass of my prayers
To call thee back. Yet let me counsel thee:
Persuade thy sister to some marriage.   40

Giovanni. Marriage? Why, that's to damn her; that's to prove
Her greedy of variety of lust.

Friar. O fearful! If thou wilt not, give me leave
To shrive her, lest she should die unabsolved.

16–17. *composition*] pronounced first with four syllables, then with five.
18. *furniture*] adornment.
21. *quintessence*] the purest essence. (Stressed on the first syllable.)
22–3. *rarely*] excellently, uniquely (not 'seldom').
28. *warned*] warned against, forbidden.
31–2. *philosophers . . . times*] pre-Christian philosophers.
32. *instance*] provide.
34. *nature . . . blind*] natural reason cannot scrutinise God's ordinances; *positions* = tenets.
40–1. *marriage*] pronounced first with three syllables, then with two.
44. *shrive her*] hear her confession.
unabsolved] unforgiven.

Giovanni. At your best leisure, father; then she'll tell you   45
How dearly she doth prize my matchless love;
Then you will know what pity 'twere we two
Should have been sundered from each other's arms.
View well her face, and in that little round
You may observe a world of variety: 50
For colour, lips, for sweet perfumes, her breath;
For jewels, eyes; for threads of purest gold,
Hair; for delicious choice of flowers, cheeks;
Wonder in every portion of that throne.
Hear her but speak, and you will swear the spheres   55
Make music to the citizens in heaven;
But father, what is else for pleasure framed,
Lest I offend your ears, shall go unnamed.
Friar. The more I hear, I pity thee the more,
That one so excellent should give those parts   60
All to a second death. What I can do
Is but to pray; and yet I could advise thee,
Wouldst thou be ruled.
Giovanni.   In what?
Friar.   Why, leave her yet.
The throne of Mercy is above your trespass;
Yet time is left you both—
Giovanni.   To embrace each other,   65
Else let all time be struck quite out of number.
She is like me, and I like her resolved.
Friar. No more, I'll visit her. This grieves me most,
Things being thus, a pair of souls are lost.   *Exeunt.*

---

54. *throne*] seat of heavenly beauty.

55–6. *the spheres / Make music*] In traditional cosmology the nine planets revolved about the earth as crystal spheres, making a divine music inaudible to mortals.

57. *what . . . framed*] the other parts of her body that are designed for pleasure.

60. *parts*] features, qualities.

61. *second death*] damnation (as in Revelation xx–xxi).

64.] i.e. 'God remains merciful despite your sin'.

65. *Yet*] still.

66. *out of number*] out of order or sequence.

[II. vi]

Enter FLORIO, DONADO, ANNABELLA, PUTANA.

Florio. Where's Giovanni?
Annabella.   Newly walked abroad,
    And, as I heard him say, gone to the friar,
    His reverend tutor.
Florio.   That's a blessèd man,
    A man made up of holiness. I hope
    He'll teach him how to gain another world.   5
Donado. [*To Annabella*] Fair gentlewoman, here's a letter sent
    To you from my young cousin; I dare swear
    He loves you in his soul. Would you could hear
    Sometimes what I see daily: sighs and tears,
    As if his breast were prison to his heart!   10
Florio. Receive it, Annabella.
Annabella.   Alas, good man!
                        [*Takes the letter.*]
Donado. [*To Putana*] What's that she said?
Putana. [*To Donado*] An 't please you, sir, she said 'Alas, good
    man!' [*Aside to him*] Truly, I do commend him to her
    every night before her first sleep, because I would have
    her dream of him; and she hearkens to that most   15
    religiously.
Donado. [*Aside to Putana*] Say'st so? Godamercy, Putana,
    there's something for thee [*Giving money*], and prithee do
    what thou canst on his behalf; sha' not be lost labour,
    take my word for 't.   20
Putana. [*Aside to Donado*] Thank you most heartily, sir. Now
    I have a feeling of your mind, let me alone to work.
Annabella. [*To Putana, offering letter*] Guardian!
Putana. Did you call?   25
Annabella. Keep this letter.
Donado. Signior Florio, in any case bid her read it instantly.

II.vi.1. *Newly walked abroad*] just gone out.
13. *An 't please*] if it please.
18. *Godamercy*] well done; many thanks.
23. *feeling*] understanding (with a play on Donado's tangible reward).

Florio. [*To Annabella*] Keep it, for what? Pray read it me here
    right.
Annabella. I shall, sir.   *She reads.*
Donado. [*To Florio*] How d'ee find her inclined, signior?   30
Florio. Troth, sir, I know not how; not all so well
    As I could wish.
Annabella. [*To Donado*] Sir, I am bound to rest your
    cousin's debtor.
    The jewel I'll return; for, if he love,
    I'll count that love a jewel.
Donado. [*To Florio*]   Mark you that?—   35
    Nay, keep them both, sweet maid.
Annabella.   You must excuse me,
    Indeed I will not keep it.
Florio. [*To Annabella*]   Where's the ring,
    That which your mother in her will bequeathed,
    And charged you on her blessing not to give 't
    To any but your husband? Send back that.   40
Annabella. I have it not.
Florio.   Ha! Have it not? Where is 't?
Annabella. My brother in the morning took it from me,
    Said he would wear 't today.
Florio.   Well, what do you say
    To young Bergetto's love? Are you content
    To match with him? Speak.
Donado.   There's the point indeed.   45
Annabella. [*Aside*] What shall I do? I must say something
    now.
Florio. What say, why d'ee not speak?
Annabella.   Sir, with your leave,
    Please you to give me freedom?
Florio.   Yes, you have 't.
Annabella. Signior Donado, if your nephew mean
    To raise his better fortunes in his match,   50
    The hope of me will hinder such a hope.
    Sir, if you love him, as I know you do,
    Find one more worthy of his choice than me.
    In short, I'm sure I sha' not be his wife.

---

47. *What say*] what do you say.

Donado. Why, here's plain dealing; I commend thee for 't,   55
And all the worst I wish thee, is heaven bless thee!
Your father yet and I will still be friends,
Shall we not, Signior Florio?
Florio.   Yes, why not?
Look, here your cousin comes.

Enter BERGETTO *and* POGGIO.

Donado. [*Aside*] O coxcomb, what doth he make here?   60
Bergetto. Where's my uncle, sirs?
Donado. What's the news now?
Bergetto. Save you, uncle, save you. You must not think I
come for nothing, masters. [*To Annabella*] And how, and
how is 't? What, you have read my letter? Ah, there I—   65
tickled you i'faith!
Poggio. [*Aside to Bergetto*] But 'twere better you had tickled
her in another place.
Bergetto. Sirrah sweetheart, I'll tell thee a good jest, and riddle
what 'tis.   70
Annabella. You say you'd tell me.
Bergetto. As I was walking just now in the street, I met a
swaggering fellow would needs take the wall of me; and
because he did thrust me, I very valiantly called him
rogue. He hereupon bade me draw; I told him I had more   75
wit than so; but when he saw that I would not, he did so
maul me with the hilts of his rapier, that my head sung
whilst my feet capered in the kennel.
Donado. [*Aside*] Was ever the like ass seen?
Annabella. And what did you all this while?   80
Bergetto. Laugh at him for a gull, till I see the blood run about
mine ears, and then I could not choose but find in my
heart to cry; till a fellow with a broad beard—they say he
is a new-come doctor—called me into this house, and

---

60. *doth he make*] is he doing.

69. *Sirrah*] usually facetious if addressed to a woman.

73. *take the wall*] London streets were narrow and drained into a central
gutter or 'kennel' (78), so the best place to walk was by the wall. To yield this
place was a courtesy; to take it was to claim superiority, sometimes with fatal
results.

81. *gull*] fool, dupe.

gave me a plaster—look you, here 'tis; and sir, there was   85
a young wench washed my face and hands most excellently. I'faith, I shall love her as long as I live for 't—did
she not, Poggio?

Poggio. Yes, and kissed him too.

Bergetto. Why la now, you think I tell a lie, uncle, I warrant.   90

Donado. Would he that beat thy blood out of thy head had
beaten some wit into it! For I fear thou never wilt have
any.

Bergetto. O, uncle, but there was a wench would have done
a man's heart good to have looked on her; by this light,   95
she had a face methinks worth twenty of you, Mistress
Annabella.

Donado. [*Aside*] Was ever such a fool born?

Annabella. I am glad she liked you, sir.

Bergetto. Are you so? By my troth, I thank you, forsooth.   100

Florio. Sure 'twas the doctor's niece, that was last day with us
here.

Bergetto. 'Twas she, 'twas she!

Donado. How do you know that, simplicity?

Bergetto. Why, does not he say so? If I should have said no, I   105
should have given him the lie, uncle, and so have de-
served a dry-beating again; I'll none of that.

Florio. A very modest, well-behaved young maid as I have
seen.

Donado. Is she indeed?   110

Florio. Indeed she is, if I have any judgement.

Donado. [*To Bergetto*] Well, sir, now you are free, you need
not care for sending letters now. You are dismissed; your
mistress here will none of you.

Bergetto. No? Why, what care I for that? I can have wenches   115
enough in Parma for half-a-crown apiece, cannot I,
Poggio?

Poggio. I'll warrant you, sir.

Donado. Signior Florio,
I thank you for your free recourse you gave   120

---

99. *liked*] probably 'pleased'.
106. *given him the lie*] called him a liar, another cause of mortal offence.
107. *dry-beating*] (a) beating that draws no blood; (b) severe beating.

For my admittance; and to you, fair maid,
That jewel I will give you 'gainst your marriage.—
Come, will you go, sir?
Bergetto. Ay, marry will I.—Mistress, farewell, mistress; I'll
come again tomorrow; farewell, mistress.   125
        Exeunt DONADO, BERGETTO *and* POGGIO.

        Enter GIOVANNI.

Florio. Son, where have you been? What, alone, alone, still,
    still?
    I would not have it so; you must forsake
    This over-bookish humour. Well, your sister
    Hath shook the fool off.
Giovanni.   'Twas no match for her.
Florio. 'Twas not indeed; I meant it nothing less.   130
    Soranzo is the man I only like;
    Look on him, Annabella. Come, 'tis supper-time,
    And it grows late.   *Exit.*
Giovanni. Whose jewel's that?
Annabella. Some sweetheart's.
Giovanni.   So I think.
Annabella.   A lusty youth,   135
    Signior Donado, gave it me to wear
    Against my marriage.
Giovanni.   But you shall not wear it;
    Send it him back again.
Annabella.   What, you are jealous?
Giovanni. That you shall know anon, at better leisure.
    Welcome, sweet night! The evening crowns the day.   140
                      Exeunt.

---

   122. *'gainst*] in anticipation of, i.e. as a wedding present given in advance
(cf. 'Against' in 137).
   128. *humour*] attitude, way of life.
   130. *meant . . . less*] didn't intend it at all.
   131. *man I only like*] man I prefer above all others.
   135. *lusty*] handsome, vigorous, 'sexy'.
   138. *jealous*] possessive and suspicious. Giovanni's reply plays on another
meaning, 'passionate'.
   140. *crowns*] (a) completes; (b) rewards.

Act III

[III. i]

Enter BERGETTO *and* POGGIO.

Bergetto. Does my uncle think to make me a baby still? No, Poggio, he shall know I have a sconce now.

Poggio. Ay, let him not bob you off like an ape with an apple.

Bergetto. 'Sfoot, I will have the wench, if he were ten uncles, in despite of his nose, Poggio.   5

Poggio. Hold him to the grindstone, and give not a jot of ground. She hath in a manner promised you already.

Bergetto. True, Poggio, and her uncle the doctor swore I should marry her.

Poggio. He swore, I remember.   10

Bergetto. And I will have her, that's more. Didst see the codpiece-point she gave me, and the box of marmalade?

Poggio. Very well, and kissed you, that my chops watered at the sight on 't. There's no way but to clap up a marriage in hugger mugger.   15

Bergetto. I will do 't, for I tell thee, Poggio, I begin to grow valiant, methinks, and my courage begins to rise.

Poggio. Should you be afraid of your uncle?

III.i.2. *sconce*] head, brain.

3. *bob you off*] put you off.

like . . . apple] by distracting you (perhaps with a sexual sense, as apes were thought of as lustful and apples as anaphrodisiacs).

4. *'Sfoot*] by God's foot.

12. *codpiece-point*] ornamental lace for tying the codpiece, a bag-like compartment in front of the breeches for accommodating the male organs.

box of marmalade] pot of preserve of any kind.

13. *chops*] chaps, jaws.

14. *clap up*] hastily arrange.

15. *in hugger mugger*] secretly.

17. *courage*] with the added meaning of 'sexual desire', continued in *rise*.

Bergetto. Hang him, old doting rascal, no. I say I will have her.
Poggio. Lose no time, then.   20
Bergetto. I will beget a race of wise men and constables, that
    shall cart whores at their own charges, and break the
    duke's peace ere I have done myself. Come away!
                                              Exeunt.

[III. ii]

        Enter FLORIO, GIOVANNI, SORANZO, ANNABELLA,
                PUTANA *and* VASQUES.

Florio. My lord Soranzo, though I must confess
    The proffers that are made me have been great
    In marriage of my daughter, yet the hope
    Of your still rising honours have prevailed
    Above all other jointures. Here she is,   5
    She knows my mind; speak for yourself to her.—
    And hear you, daughter, see you use him nobly.
    For any private speech I'll give you time.—
    Come, son, and you the rest, let them alone,
    Agree as they may.
Soranzo.   I thank you, sir.   10
Giovanni. [*Aside to Annabella*] Sister, be not all woman; think
    on me.
Soranzo. Vasques!
Vasques. My lord?
Soranzo. Attend me without.
        Exeunt omnes; manent SORANZO *and* ANNABELLA.
Annabella.   Sir, what's your will with me?

---

21. *constables*] traditionally represented as slow-witted.
22. *cart whores*] Whores were punished by being paraded in carts, or
whipped as they walked behind the cart.
    at their own charges] (a) at their own expense; (b) on their own account.
22–3. *break . . . peace*] create a riotous disturbance.
23. *ere . . . myself*] before I have finished breaking the peace myself.

III.ii.5. *jointures*] (a) unions; (b) proffered marriage settlements (perhaps a
reference to Donado's offer at I.iii.14–18).
  11. *all woman*] altogether a woman, i.e. faithless.
  14.] Wait for me outside.
  14.1.S.D.] Literally, 'All leave; Soranzo and Annabella remain'.

Soranzo. Do you not know what I should tell you?
Annabella. Yes, 15
    You'll say you love me.
Soranzo.   And I'll swear it, too.
    Will you believe it?
Annabella.   'Tis not point of faith.

Enter GIOVANNI *above.*

Soranzo. Have you not will to love?
Annabella.   Not you.
Soranzo.   Whom, then?
Annabella. That's as the Fates infer.
Giovanni. [*Aside*] Of those I'm regent now.
Soranzo.   What mean you, sweet? 20
Annabella. To live and die a maid.
Soranzo.   O, that's unfit.
Giovanni. [*Aside*] Here's one can say that's but a woman's
    note.
Soranzo. Did you but see my heart, then would you swear—
Annabella. That you were dead.
Giovanni. [*Aside*]   That's true, or somewhat near it.
Soranzo. See you these true love's tears?
Annabella.   No.
Giovanni. [*Aside*]   Now she winks. 25
Soranzo. They plead to you for grace.
Annabella.   Yet nothing speak.
Soranzo. O, grant my suit!
Annabella.   What is 't?
Soranzo.   To let me live—
Annabella. Take it.
Soranzo.   —still yours.
Annabella.   That is not mine to give.

---

15. *what I should tell*] what I'm going to tell.

17. *point of faith*] an essential article of doctrine.

17.1.S.D. *above*] i.e. on the upper stage. This scene and the next two take place in Florio's house, and Giovanni may be imagined as eavesdropping from the gallery overlooking a salon or hall.

19. *infer*] bring about.

22. *note*] (a) tune; (b) defining characteristic ('a typical piece of feminine hypocrisy').

25. *winks*] closes both eyes.

Giovanni. [*Aside*] One such another word would kill his
    hopes.
Soranzo. Mistress, to leave those fruitless strifes of wit,   30
    I know I have loved you long, and loved you truly.
    Not hope of what you have, but what you are
    Have drawn me on. Then let me not in vain
    Still feel the rigour of your chaste disdain.
    I'm sick, and sick to th' heart.
Annabella.   Help, aqua-vitae!   35
Soranzo. What mean you?
Annabella.   Why, I thought you had been sick!
Soranzo. Do you mock my love?
Giovanni. [*Aside*]   There, sir, she was too nimble.
Soranzo. [*Aside*] 'Tis plain, she laughs at me!—These
    scornful taunts
    Neither become your modesty or years.
Annabella. You are no looking-glass, or if you were   40
    I'd dress my language by you.
Giovanni. [*Aside*]   I'm confirmed.
Annabella. To put you out of doubt, my lord, methinks
    Your common sense should make you understand
    That if I loved you, or desired your love,
    Some way I should have given you better taste;   45
    But since you are a nobleman, and one
    I would not wish should spend his youth in hopes,
    Let me advise you here to forbear your suit,
    And think I wish you well; I tell you this.
Soranzo. Is 't you speak this?
Annabella.   Yes, I myself. Yet know—   50
    Thus far I give you comfort—if mine eyes
    Could have picked out a man amongst all those
    That sued to me, to make a husband of,
    You should have been that man; let this suffice.

---

29. *One such another word*] another remark like that.
35. *aqua-vitae*] brandy or other spirits.
41. *dress*] arrange, correct.
45. *better taste*] a hint of my better feeling.
51–4. *if mine . . . that man*] Here and in 61–2 Annabella is probably expressing contempt under the guise of a compliment: Soranzo would be the
fittest suitor to be made a convenience and a cuckold of.

    Be noble in your secrecy, and wise.   55
Giovanni. [*Aside*] Why, now I see she loves me.
Annabella.   One word more:
    As ever virtue lived within your mind,
    As ever noble courses were your guide,
    As ever you would have me know you loved me,
    Let not my father know hereof by you: 60
    If I hereafter find that I must marry,
    It shall be you or none.
Soranzo.   I take that promise.
Annabella. O, O my head!
Soranzo.   What's the matter? Not well?
Annabella. O, I begin to sicken!
Giovanni. [*Aside*]   Heaven forbid!
                            Exit from above.
Soranzo. Help, help, within there, ho!   65
    Look to your daughter, Signior Florio.

         Enter FLORIO, GIOVANNI, PUTANA.

Florio. Hold her up! She swoons.
Giovanni. Sister, how d'ee?
Annabella.   Sick, brother. Are you there?
Florio. Convey her to her bed instantly, whilst I send for a
    physician. Quickly, I say.   70
Putana. Alas, poor child!   *Exeunt; manet* SORANZO.

         Enter VASQUES.

Vasques. My lord.
Soranzo. Oh, Vasques, now I doubly am undone,
    Both in my present and my future hopes!
    She plainly told me that she could not love,   75
    And thereupon soon sickened, and I fear
    Her life's in danger.
Vasques. [*Aside*] By 'r Lady sir, and so is yours, if you knew
    all. [*Aloud*] 'Las, sir, I am sorry for that; may be 'tis but
    the maid's sickness, an overflux of youth—and then, sir, 80

---

80. *maid's sickness*] chlorosis, a form of anaemia in young women, thought
to be caused by the need for a man.
   overflux] excess (see III.iv.8 and note).

there is no such present remedy as present marriage. But
hath she given you an absolute denial?

Soranzo. She hath and she hath not. I'm full of grief,
But what she said I'll tell thee as we go.   *Exeunt.*

[III. iii]

Enter GIOVANNI *and* PUTANA.

Putana. O sir, we are all undone, quite undone, utterly undone, and shamed forever; your sister, O your sister!

Giovanni. What of her? For heaven's sake speak, how does
she?

Putana. O, that ever I was born to see this day!   5

Giovanni. She is not dead, ha, is she?

Putana. Dead! No, she is quick; 'tis worse, she is with child.
You know what you have done, heaven forgive 'ee! 'Tis
too late to repent, now heaven help us!

Giovanni. With child? How dost thou know 't?   10

Putana. How do I know 't? Am I at these years ignorant what
the meanings of qualms and water-pangs be? Of changing
of colours, queasiness of stomachs, pukings, and another
thing that I could name? Do not, for her and your credit's
sake, spend the time in asking how and which way 'tis so.   15
She is quick, upon my word; if you let a physician see her
water y' are undone.

Giovanni. But in what case is she?

Putana. Prettily amended. 'Twas but a fit, which I soon
espied, and she must look for often henceforward.   20

Giovanni. Commend me to her, bid her take no care;
Let not the doctor visit her, I charge you;
Make some excuse till I return.—O me,
I have a world of business in my head!
Do not discomfort her.—   25
How do this news perplex me! If my father
Come to her, tell him she's recovered well;

III.iii.7. *quick*] (a) alive; (b) pregnant.
12. *water-pangs*] frequent need to urinate.
13–14. *another thing*] Menstruation has ceased.
18. *case*] state.
19. *Prettily amended*] pretty well better.
21. *take no care*] not to worry.

Say 'twas but some ill diet. D'ee hear, woman,
Look you to 't.
Putana. I will, sir.   *Exeunt.*

                                                              30

[III. iv]

                Enter FLORIO *and* RICHARDETTO.

Florio. And how d'ee find her, sir?
Richardetto.   Indifferent well:
I see no danger, scarce perceive she's sick,
But that she told me she had lately eaten
Melons, and, as she thought, those disagreed
With her young stomach.
Florio.   Did you give her aught?
Richardetto. An easy surfeit-water, nothing else.   5
You need not doubt her health; I rather think
Her sickness is a fullness of her blood—
You understand me?
Florio.   I do; you counsel well,
And once within these few days will so order 't
She shall be married, ere she know the time.   10
Richardetto. Yet let not haste, sir, make unworthy choice;
That were dishonour.
Florio.   Master doctor, no,
I will not do so neither. In plain words,
My lord Soranzo is the man I mean.
Richardetto. A noble and a virtuous gentleman.   15
Florio. As any is in Parma. Not far hence
Dwells Father Bonaventure, a grave friar,
Once tutor to my son; now at his cell
I'll have 'em married.
Richardetto.   You have plotted wisely.
Florio. I'll send one straight to speak with him tonight. 20

III.iv.1. *Indifferent well*] tolerably well.

6. *surfeit-water*] medicine to correct excess.

8. *a fullness of her blood*] Blood was considered the seat of sexual appetite in women; its 'fullness' indicated readiness for sexual intercourse, and abstinence could then cause morbid melancholy, the 'falling-sickness', and other maladies.

16–17. *A noble . . . Parma*] Richardetto's words are consciously ironical, Florio's unconsciously so.

Richardetto. Soranzo's wise; he will delay no time.
Florio. It shall be so.

Enter Friar *and* GIOVANNI.

Friar.   Good peace be here and love!
Florio. Welcome, religious friar. You are one
    That still bring blessing to the place you come to.   25
Giovanni. Sir, with what speed I could, I did my best
    To draw this holy man from forth his cell
    To visit my sick sister, that with words
    Of ghostly comfort in this time of need
    He might absolve her, whether she live or die.   30
Florio. 'Twas well done, Giovanni; thou herein
    Hast showed a Christian's care, a brother's love.
    Come, father, I'll conduct you to her chamber,
    And one thing would entreat you.
Friar.   Say on, sir.
Florio. I have a father's dear impression,   35
    And wish, before I fall into my grave,
    That I might see her married, as 'tis fit;
    A word from you, grave man, will win her more
    Than all our best persuasions.
Friar.   Gentle sir,
    All this I'll say, that heaven may prosper her.   40
Exeunt.

[III. v]

Enter GRIMALDI.

Grimaldi. Now if the doctor keep his word, Soranzo,
    Twenty to one you miss your bride. I know
    'Tis an unnoble act, and not becomes

---

    25. *still*] always.
    29. *ghostly*] spiritual.
    30. *absolve her*] hear her confession.
    35. *a father's dear impression*] probably 'the imprinted likeness of my own dear father (which I wish to see passed on to another generation)'.

A soldier's valour; but in terms of love,
Where merit cannot sway, policy must.   5
I am resolved, if this physician
Play not on both hands, then Soranzo falls.

Enter RICHARDETTO [*with a box*].

Richardetto. You are come as I could wish: this very night
    Soranzo, 'tis ordained, must be affied
    To Annabella, and, for aught I know,   10
    Married.
Grimaldi.   How!
Richardetto.   Yet your patience.
    The place, 'tis Friar Bonaventure's cell.
    Now I would wish you to bestow this night
    In watching thereabouts; 'tis but a night;
    If you miss now! Tomorrow I'll know all.   15
Grimaldi. Have you the poison?
Richardetto.   Here 'tis in this box.
    Doubt nothing, this will do 't; in any case,
    As you respect your life, be quick and sure.
Grimaldi. I'll speed him.
Richardetto.   Do; away, for 'tis not safe
    You should be seen much here; ever my love.   20
Grimaldi. And mine to you.   *Exit.*
Richardetto. So, if this hit, I'll laugh and hug revenge;
    And they that now dream of a wedding-feast
    May chance to mourn the lusty bridegroom's ruin.
    But to my other business.—Niece Philotis!   25

Enter PHILOTIS.

  III.v.4. *terms*] circumstances.
  5. *policy*] calculation, cunning.
  7. *Play not on both hands*] is not deceiving me, double-dealing.
  9. *affied*] betrothed.
  12. *Friar Bonaventure's cell*] Richardetto is remembering what Florio has
said at III.iv.19–20; but in the event the betrothal takes place in Annabella's
chamber (III.vi), and Grimaldi is misled with fatal results.
  19. *speed*] dispatch.
  22. *hit*] succeed.
  hug] embrace with joy.

Philotis. Uncle?

Richardetto.   My lovely niece, you have bethought 'ee?

Philotis. Yes, and, as you counselled,
    Fashioned my heart to love him; but he swears
    He will tonight be married, for he fears
    His uncle else, if he should know the drift,
    Will hinder all, and call his coz to shrift.   30

Richardetto. Tonight? Why, best of all. But let me see,
    Ay—ha—yes,—so it shall be: in disguise
    We'll early to the friar's; I have thought on 't.

Enter BERGETTO *and* POGGIO.

Philotis. Uncle, he comes!

Richardetto.   Welcome, my worthy coz.   35

Bergetto. Lass, pretty lass, come buss, lass. [*Kisses her.*] Aha,
    Poggio!

Philotis. There's hope of this yet.

Richardetto. You shall have time enough; withdraw a little.
    We must confer at large.   40

Bergetto. Have you not sweetmeats or dainty devices for me?

Philotis. You shall enough, sweetheart.

Bergetto. Sweetheart! Mark that, Poggio. By my troth I cannot
    choose but kiss thee once more for that word 'sweet-
    heart'. [*Kisses her.*] Poggio, I have a monstrous swelling   45
    about my stomach, whatsoever the matter be.

Poggio. You shall have physic for 't, sir.

Richardetto. Time runs apace.

Bergetto. Time's a blockhead! [*Kisses her.*]

Richardetto. Be ruled: when we have done what's fit to do,   50
    Then you may kiss your fill, and bed her too.   *Exeunt.*

---

28. *Fashioned*] managed, disciplined.
him] Bergetto.
30. *drift*] intention.
31. *call . . . to shrift*] call his kinsman (Bergetto) to account.
32. *best of all*] all the better.
36. *buss*] kiss.
40. *at large*] (a) fully; (b) together ('This is no time for a *tête-à-tête*').
45. *swelling*] with a sexual implication.

[III. vi]

Enter the Friar *in his study, sitting in a chair,* ANNABELLA
*kneeling and whispering to him, a table before them and wax lights;
she weeps, and wrings her hands.*

Friar. I am glad to see this penance; for believe me,
    You have unripped a soul so foul and guilty,
    As I must tell you true, I marvel how
    The earth hath borne you up. But weep, weep on;
    These tears may do you good. Weep faster yet,   5
    Whiles I do read a lecture.
Annabella.   Wretched creature!
Friar. Ay, you are wretched, miserably wretched,
    Almost condemned alive. There is a place—
    List, daughter!—in a black and hollow vault,
    Where day is never seen; there shines no sun,   10
    But flaming horror of consuming fires;
    A lightless sulphur, choked with smoky fogs
    Of an infected darkness. In this place
    Dwell many thousand thousand sundry sorts
    Of never-dying deaths: there damnèd souls   15
    Roar without pity, there are gluttons fed
    With toads and adders; there is burning oil
    Poured down the drunkard's throat; the usurer
    Is forced to sup whole draughts of molten gold;
    There is the murderer for ever stabbed,   20
    Yet can he never die; there lies the wanton
    On racks of burning steel, whiles in his soul
    He feels the torment of his raging lust.
Annabella. Mercy, O mercy!
Friar.   There stands these wretched things
    Who have dreamt out whole years in lawless sheets   25

III.vi.0.1.S.D. *in his study*] The Friar and Annabella are seemingly disclosed in the discovery space backstage. Apparently they are still in her
chamber (see III.iv.33); Soranzo has returned to the house and is waiting
below (III.vi.44).
   2. *unripped*] laid open.
   6. *read a lecture*] expound your sins; deliver a reprimand.
   11. *horror*] literally 'bristling', suggesting the flames and their movement.
   13. *infected*] poisoned, filled with corruption.

And secret incests, cursing one another.
Then you will wish each kiss your brother gave
Had been a dagger's point; then you shall hear
How he will cry, 'O, would my wicked sister
Had first been damned, when she did yield to lust!'   30
But soft, methinks I see repentance work
New motions in your heart; say, how is 't with you?
Annabella. Is there no way left to redeem my miseries?
Friar. There is, despair not: heaven is merciful,
And offers grace even now. 'Tis thus agreed,   35
First, for your honour's safety that you marry
The Lord Soranzo; next, to save your soul,
Leave off this life, and henceforth live to him.
Annabella. Ay me!
Friar.   Sigh not, I know the baits of sin
Are hard to leave; O, 'tis a death to do 't.   40
Remember what must come! Are you content?
Annabella. I am.
Friar.   I like it well; we'll take the time.
Who's near us there?

                    Enter FLORIO, GIOVANNI.

Florio.   Did you call, father?
Friar. Is Lord Soranzo come?
Florio.   He stays below.
Friar. Have you acquainted him at full?
Florio.   I have,   45
And he is overjoyed.
Friar.   And so are we;
Bid him come near.
Giovanni. [*Aside*]   My sister weeping, ha!
I fear this friar's falsehood. [*To them*] I will call him.
                                                  Exit.

Florio. Daughter, are you resolved?
Annabella.   Father, I am.

          Enter GIOVANNI, SORANZO *and* VASQUES.

---

32. *motions*] stirrings.
38. *live to him*] devote yourself to him.
42. *the time*] the favourable moment. The Friar decides not to have the ceremony performed later in his cell, but immediately, while Annabella is willing.

Florio. My lord Soranzo, here   50
    Give me your hand; for that I give you this.
                        [Joins their hands.]
Soranzo. Lady, say you so too?
Annabella.   I do, and vow
    To live with you and yours.
Friar.   Timely resolved.
    My blessing rest on both! More to be done,
    You may perform it on the morning sun.   *Exeunt.*   55

[III. vii]

    Enter GRIMALDI *with his rapier drawn, and a dark lantern.*

Grimaldi. 'Tis early night as yet, and yet too soon
    To finish such a work; here I will lie
    To listen who comes next.   *He lies down.*

      Enter BERGETTO *and* PHILOTIS *disguised, and after*
              RICHARDETTO *and* POGGIO.

Bergetto. We are almost at the place I hope, sweetheart.
Grimaldi. [*Aside*] I hear them near, and heard one say
    'sweetheart';   5
    'Tis he. Now guide my hand, some angry Justice,
    Home to his bosom. [*Aloud*] Now, have at you, sir!
                 Strikes Bergetto and exit.
Bergetto. O, help, help, here's a stitch fallen in my guts; O, for
    a flesh-tailor quickly!—Poggio!
Philotis. What ails my love?   10
Bergetto. I am sure I cannot piss forward and backward, and
    yet I am wet before and behind. Lights, lights, ho, lights!
Philotis. Alas, some villain here has slain my love!

    51–3.] the stage equivalent of a formal betrothal, in which each party gives
a legally binding promise to marry the other.

    III.vii.0.1.S.D. dark lantern] a lantern that could be kept burning while its
light was concealed by a shutter.
    2–3. *I will . . . listen*] Grimaldi puts his ear to the ground to detect ap-
proaching footfalls.
    6. *angry Justice*] spirit carrying out retribution.
    8. *here's a stitch fallen*] a stitch has burst; hence the call for a 'flesh-tailor',
i.e. a surgeon.

Richardetto. O, heaven forbid it! Raise up the next
    neighbours
    Instantly, Poggio, and bring lights.   *Exit* POGGIO.   15
    How is 't, Bergetto? Slain? It cannot be;
    Are you sure y' are hurt?
Bergetto. O, my belly seethes like a porridge-pot; some cold
    water, I shall boil over else. My whole body is in a sweat,
    that you may wring my shirt; feel here—why, Poggio!   20

    Enter POGGIO *with* Officers, *and lights and halberts.*

Poggio. Here; alas, how do you?
Richardetto. Give me a light—what's here? All blood! O sirs,
    Signior Donado's nephew now is slain!
    Follow the murderer with all the haste
    Up to the city; he cannot be far hence.   25
    Follow, I beseech you.
Officer.   Follow, follow, follow!
                              Exeunt Officers.
Richardetto. Tear off thy linen, coz, to stop his wounds.—
    Be of good comfort, man.
Bergetto. Is all this mine own blood? Nay then, goodnight with
    me. Poggio, commend me to my uncle, dost hear? Bid   30
    him for my sake make much of this wench—O, I am
    going the wrong way sure, my belly aches so—O, fare-
    well, Poggio—O——O——   *Dies.*
Philotis. O, he is dead!
Poggio.   How! Dead?
Richardetto.   He's dead indeed.
    'Tis now too late to weep; let's have him home,   35
    And with what speed we may find out the murderer.
Poggio. O my master, my master, my master!   *Exeunt.*

---

14. *next*] nearest.
20.1.S.D. halberts] weapons of a watch or civic guard, combining spear
with axe.
24. *all the haste*] all possible haste.
27. *coz*] cousin, i.e. niece. (Addressed to Philotis.)
31. *make much of*] take care of, be generous to.
32. *going the wrong way*] dying.

[III. viii]

Enter VASQUES *and* HIPPOLITA.

Hippolita. Betrothed?
Vasques. I saw it.
Hippolita. And when's the marriage day?
Vasques.   Some two days hence.
Hippolita. Two days? Why, man, I would but wish two hours
    To send him to his last and lasting sleep;
    And Vasques, thou shalt see, I'll do it bravely.   5
Vasques. I do not doubt your wisdom, nor, I trust, you my
    secrecy. I am infinitely yours.
Hippolita. I will be thine in spite of my disgrace.
    So soon? O wicked man, I durst be sworn
    He'd laugh to see me weep.   10
Vasques. And that's a villainous fault in him.
Hippolita. No, let him laugh; I'm armed in my resolves,
    Be thou still true.
Vasques. I should get little by treachery against so hopeful a
    preferment as I am like to climb to.   15
Hippolita. Even to my bosom, Vasques; let my youth
    Revel in these new pleasures. If we thrive,
    He now hath but a pair of days to live.   *Exeunt.*

[III. ix]

Enter FLORIO, DONADO, RICHARDETTO,
POGGIO *and* Officers.

Florio. 'Tis bootless now to show yourself a child,
    Signior Donado; what is done, is done.
    Spend not the time in tears, but seek for justice.
Richardetto. I must confess, somewhat I was in fault,

III.viii.6. *bravely*] finely.
16. *preferment*] promotion.
  like] likely.
17. *my youth*] either a contemptuous reference to Soranzo ('Let the young man enjoy his new love while he can'), or to Hippolita's own youth, to be renewed by taking Vasques to her bosom.

III.ix.1. *bootless*] useless.

That had not first acquainted you what love   5
Passed 'twixt him and my niece; but as I live,
His fortune grieves me as it were mine own.
Donado. Alas, poor creature, he meant no man harm,
That I am sure of.
Florio.   I believe that too.
But stay, my masters, are you sure you saw   10
The murderer pass here?
Officer. An it please you sir, we are sure we saw a ruffian, with
a naked weapon in his hand all bloody, get into my lord
Cardinal's grace's gate, that we are sure of; but for fear of
his grace, bless us! [*Crossing themselves*] we durst go no   15
further.
Donado. Know you what manner of man he was?
Officer. Yes, sure I know the man, they say 'a is a soldier; he
that loved your daughter, sir, an 't please ye, 'twas he for
certain.   20
Florio. Grimaldi, on my life!
Officer.   Ay, ay, the same.
Richardetto. The Cardinal is noble; he no doubt
Will give true justice.
Donado. Knock someone at the gate.
Poggio. I'll knock, sir.   *Poggio knocks.*   25
Servant. (*Within*) What would 'ee?
Florio. We require speech with the lord Cardinal
About some present business; pray inform
His grace that we are here.

Enter Cardinal *and* GRIMALDI.

Cardinal. Why, how now, friends! What saucy mates are you   30
That know nor duty nor civility?

---

12. *An it please you*] if you please.

15.S.D.] first supplied in the Revels Plays edition to suit the words 'bless
us!' and the dread of the Cardinal they express.

26. *What would 'ee*] an unceremonious form of words, remarkable as
coming from a servant: 'thee', contracted here, was used for inferiors and
intimates.

28. *present*] urgent.

30. *saucy mates*] impudent low fellows.

31. *nor . . . nor*] neither . . . nor.

Are we a person fit to be your host?
Or is our house become your common inn,
To beat our doors at pleasure? What such haste
Is yours, as that it cannot wait fit times?   35
Are you the masters of this commonwealth,
And know no more discretion? O, your news
Is here before you; you have lost a nephew,
Donado, last night by Grimaldi slain.
Is that your business? Well, sir, we have knowledge on 't;   40
Let that suffice.
Grimaldi.   In presence of your grace,
In thought I never meant Bergetto harm;
But Florio, you can tell, with how much scorn
Soranzo backed with his confederates
Hath often wronged me. I to be revenged—   45
For that I could not win him else to fight—
Had thought by way of ambush to have killed him,
But was unluckily therein mistook;
Else he had felt what late Bergetto did.
And though my fault to him were merely chance,   50
Yet humbly I submit me to your grace,   *[Kneeling]*
To do with me as you please.
Cardinal.   Rise up, Grimaldi.
                               [He rises.]
You citizens of Parma, if you seek
For justice: know, as nuncio from the Pope,
For this offence I here receive Grimaldi   55
Into his Holiness' protection.
He is no common man, but nobly born,
Of princes' blood, though you, sir Florio,
Thought him too mean a husband for your daughter.
If more you seek for, you must go to Rome,   60
For he shall thither. Learn more wit, for shame.

---

32. *Are we a person*] the quasi-regal 'we'.
34. *What such*] what kind of.
36. *masters of this commonwealth*] magistrates of the community.
48.] For this mistake, see III.v.12 and note.
49. *late*] just now.
59. *mean*] of low rank or status; with irony, as the 'nobly born' Grimaldi
ranks much higher in the social scale than Florio.

Bury your dead.—Away, Grimaldi; leave 'em.

Exeunt Cardinal *and* GRIMALDI.

Donado. Is this a churchman's voice? Dwells Justice here?

Florio. Justice is fled to heaven and comes no nearer.

    Soranzo, was 't for him? O impudence! 65
    Had he the face to speak it, and not blush?
    Come, come, Donado, there's no help in this,
    When cardinals think murder's not amiss.
    Great men may do their wills; we must obey,
    But heaven will judge them for 't another day. *Exeunt.* 70

64.] Astraea, goddess of justice, dwelt among men in the golden age, but was driven away by the crimes of the iron age and became the constellation Virgo.

Act IV

A banquet. Hautboys. Enter the Friar, GIOVANNI,
ANNABELLA, PHILOTIS, SORANZO, DONADO, FLORIO,
RICHARDETTO, PUTANA *and* VASQUES.

Friar. These holy rites performed, now take your times,
    To spend the remnant of the day in feast;
    Such fit repasts are pleasing to the saints
    Who are your guests, though not with mortal eyes
    To be beheld. Long prosper in this day,   5
    You happy couple, to each other's joy!
Soranzo. Father, your prayer is heard. The hand of goodness
    Hath been a shield for me against my death,
    And, more to bless me, hath enriched my life
    With this most precious jewel—such a prize   10
    As earth hath not another like to this.
    Cheer up, my love—and gentlemen, my friends,
    Rejoice with me in mirth: this day we'll crown
    With lusty cups to Annabella's health.
Giovanni. (*Aside*) O, torture! Were the marriage yet undone,   15
    Ere I'd endure this sight, to see my love
    Clipped by another, I would dare confusion,
    And stand the horror of ten thousand deaths.

IV.i.0.1.S.D. A banquet] This could mean providing anything from wine
(which traditionally followed a wedding) to a full-scale feast; *repasts* in 3
suggests that some food is being offered.
    Hautboys] oboes.
    3. *saints*] souls of the faithful.
    5. *Long . . . day*] may this day prove fortunate, and may you long prosper
in this marriage.
    14. *lusty cups*] cups of strong wine.
    17. *Clipped*] embraced.
    confusion] destruction, damnation.

Vasques. Are you not well, sir?

Giovanni.   Prithee, fellow, wait.

    I need not thy officious diligence.   20

Florio. Signior Donado, come, you must forget

    Your late mishaps, and drown your cares in wine.

Soranzo. Vasques!

Vasques.   My lord?

Soranzo.   Reach me that weighty bowl.

    Here, brother Giovanni, here's to you;

    Your turn comes next, though now a bachelor: 25

    Here's to your sister's happiness and mine!

                    [Drinks, and offers him the bowl.]

Giovanni. I cannot drink.

Soranzo.   What?

Giovanni.   'Twill indeed offend me.

Annabella. [*To Soranzo*] Pray, do not urge him if he be not

    willing.   *Hautboys.*

Florio. How now, what noise is this?

Vasques. O sir, I had forgot to tell you: certain young maidens   30

    of Parma, in honour to Madam Annabella's marriage,

    have sent their loves to her in a masque, for which they

    humbly crave your patience and silence.

Soranzo. We are much bound to them, so much the more

    As it comes unexpected; guide them in.   35

      Enter HIPPOLITA *and* Ladies *in white robes* [*all masked*],
          with garlands of willows. Music, and a dance.

    Thanks, lovely virgins. Now might we but know

    To whom we have been beholding for this love,

    We shall acknowledge it.

Hippolita.   Yes, you shall know.

                          [Unmasks.]

    What think you now?

Omnes.   Hippolita!

Hippolita.   'Tis she,

    Be not amazed; nor blush, young lovely bride.   40

---

19. *wait*] get on with your business of serving.

27. *offend*] upset.

37. *beholding*] beholden.

love] act of kindness.

I come not to defraud you of your man.
[*To Soranzo*] 'Tis now no time to reckon up the talk
What Parma long hath rumoured of us both.
Let rash report run on; the breath that vents it
Will, like a bubble, break itself at last.   45
[*To Annabella*] But now to you, sweet creature; lend 's
    your hand.
Perhaps it hath been said that I would claim
Some interest in Soranzo, now your lord.
What I have right to do, his soul knows best;
But in my duty to your noble worth,   50
Sweet Annabella, and my care of you,
Here take, Soranzo, take this hand from me.
I'll once more join what by the holy Church
                    [*She joins their hands*]
Is finished and allowed. Have I done well?

Soranzo. You have too much engaged us.

Hippolita.   One thing more: 55
That you may know my single charity,
Freely I here remit all interest
I e'er could claim, and give you back your vows;
And to confirm 't—reach me a cup of wine—
My lord Soranzo, in this draught I drink   60
Long rest t'ee! [*Aside to Vasques*] Look to it, Vasques.

Vasques. [*Aside to Hippolita*] Fear nothing.
               He gives her a poisoned cup; she drinks.

Soranzo. Hippolita, I thank you, and will pledge
This happy union as another life.—
Wine there!   65

Vasques. You shall have none, neither shall you pledge her.

Hippolita. How!

Vasques. Know now, mistress she-devil, your own mischie-
vous treachery hath killed you; I must not marry you.

---

43. *What*] that.
54. *allowed*] approved.
55. *engaged us*] put us in your debt: 'You are too kind.'
56. *single charity*] sincere love.
57. *remit*] renounce.
interest] concern, claim.
64. *union*] accord, agreement.
69. *must not*] am not destined to.

Hippolita. Villain!   70

Omnes. What's the matter?

Vasques. Foolish woman, thou art now like a firebrand, that hath kindled others and burnt thyself. *Troppo sperar, inganna.* Thy vain hope hath deceived thee; thou art but dead. If thou hast any grace, pray.   75

Hippolita. Monster!

Vasques. Die in charity, for shame!—This thing of malice, this woman, had privately corrupted me with promise of marriage, under this politic reconciliation to poison my lord, whiles she might laugh at his confusion on his marriage   80 day. I promised her fair, but I knew what my reward should have been; and would willingly have spared her life, but that I was acquainted with the danger of her disposition—and now have fitted her a just payment in her own coin. There she is, she hath yet——and end thy   85 days in peace, vile woman. As for life, there's no hope; think not on 't.

Omnes. Wonderful justice!

Richardetto.   Heaven, thou art righteous.

Hippolita. O, 'tis true,

    I feel my minute coming. Had that slave   90
    Kept promise—O, my torment!—thou this hour
    Hadst died, Soranzo.—Heat above hell-fire!—
    Yet ere I pass away—cruel, cruel flames!—
    Take here my curse amongst you: may thy bed
    Of marriage be a rack unto thy heart—   95
    Burn, blood, and boil in vengeance; O my heart,
    My flame's intolerable!—May'st thou live
    To father bastards; may her womb bring forth
    Monsters, and die together in your sins
    Hated, scorned and unpitied!—O—O—   *Dies.* 100

Florio. Was e'er so vile a creature?

Richardetto.   Here's the end

73–4. *Troppo sperar, inganna*] Too much hoping deceives.

79. *politic*] cunning.

82. *should*] would.

85. *yet* ——] The two long dashes in the quarto may represent indecipherable words in the MS; or *yet* may be a misreading of 'it'.

90. *minute*] appointed moment.

Of lust and pride.
Annabella.   It is a fearful sight.
Soranzo. Vasques, I know thee now a trusty servant,
      And never will forget thee.—Come, my love,
      We'll home, and thank the heavens for this escape.—   105
      Father and friends, we must break up this mirth;
      It is too sad a feast.
Donado.   Bear hence the body.
Friar. [*Aside to Giovanni*] Here's an ominous change;
      Mark this, my Giovanni, and take heed!
      I fear the event: that marriage seldom's good   110
      Where the bride-banquet so begins in blood.   *Exeunt.*

[IV. ii]

Enter RICHARDETTO *and* PHILOTIS.

Richardetto. My wretched wife, more wretched in her shame
      Than in her wrongs to me, hath paid too soon
      The forfeit of her modesty and life.
      And I am sure, my niece, though vengeance hover,
      Keeping aloof yet from Soranzo's fall,   5
      Yet he will fall, and sink with his own weight.
      I need not—now my heart persuades me so—
      To further his confusion. There is One
      Above begins to work; for, as I hear,
      Debates already 'twixt his wife and him   10
      Thicken and run to head. She, as 'tis said,
      Slightens his love, and he abandons hers;
      Much talk I hear. Since things go thus, my niece,
      In tender love and pity of your youth,
      My counsel is that you should free your years   15
      From hazard of these woes, by flying hence
      To fair Cremona, there to vow your soul
      In holiness a holy votaress;

---

110. *event*] outcome.

IV.ii.3.] i.e. 'the penalty (for the wrong she did me) of disgrace and death'.
11. *Thicken . . . head*] multiply and draw to a crisis.
12. *Slightens*] treats with indifference.
18. *votaress*] nun.

Leave me to see the end of these extremes.
All human worldly courses are uneven;   20
  No life is blessèd but the way to heaven.
Philotis. Uncle, shall I resolve to be a nun?
Richardetto. Ay, gentle niece, and in your hourly prayers
  Remember me, your poor unhappy uncle.
  Hie to Cremona now, as fortune leads,   25
  Your home your cloister, your best friends your beads.
  Your chaste and single life shall crown your birth;
  Who dies a virgin lives a saint on earth.
Philotis. Then farewell world, and worldly thoughts adieu!
  Welcome, chaste vows; myself I yield to you.   30

                        Exeunt.

[IV. iii]

     Enter SORANZO *unbraced* [*with a drawn sword*],
         and ANNABELLA *dragged in.*

Soranzo. Come, strumpet, famous whore! Were every drop
  Of blood that runs in thy adulterous veins
  A life, this sword—dost see 't?—should in one blow
  Confound them all. Harlot, rare, notable harlot,
  That with thy brazen face maintain'st thy sin,   5
  Was there no man in Parma to be bawd
  To your loose cunning whoredom else but I?
  Must your hot itch and plurisy of lust,
  The heyday of your luxury, be fed

---

    19. *extremes*] violent actions or sufferings.
    25. *Hie*] go quickly.
    26. *beads*] rosary.
    27. *crown*] fulfil, honour.
    28. *Who*] she who.

  IV.iii.0.1.S.D. unbraced] with part of clothing unfastened or removed;
probably Soranzo's doublet is unbuttoned.
    4. *Confound*] destroy.
  rare (a) exceptional; (b) excellent (ironically; cf. IV.iii.25).
    5. *maintain'st*] (a) defends; (b) perseveres in.
    6. *bawd*] brothel-keeper or pander.
    8. *plurisy*] superabundance.
    9. *heyday*] excitement.
  luxury] lecherousness.

                                                                    10
Up to a surfeit, and could none but I
Be picked out to be cloak to your close tricks,
Your belly-sports? Now I must be the dad
To all that gallimaufry that's stuffed
In thy corrupted bastard-bearing womb?
Why must I?
Annabella.   Beastly man, why, 'tis thy fate.   15
I sued not to thee, for, but that I thought
Your over-loving lordship would have run
Mad on denial, had ye lent me time,
I would have told 'ee in what case I was;
But you would needs be doing.
Soranzo.   Whore of whores!   20
Darest thou tell me this?
Annabella.   O yes, why not?
You were deceived in me: 'twas not for love
I chose you, but for honour. Yet know this:
Would you be patient yet, and hide your shame,
I'd see whether I could love you.
Soranzo.   Excellent quean!   25
Why, art thou not with child?
Annabella.   What needs all this,
When 'tis superfluous? I confess I am.
Soranzo. Tell me by whom.
Annabella.   Soft, sir, 'twas not in my bargain.
Yet somewhat, sir, to stay your longing stomach

---

11. *close*] (a) secret; (b) physically close.

tricks] (a) habits; (b) games; (c) techniques.

13. *gallimaufry*] confused jumble.

15. *Why*] The quarto text reads 'Shey' at the start of a page, but the catchword (set at the foot of the previous page to guide the printer) reads 'Say', corrected in one copy to 'Why'. 'Shey' occurs in five other Elizabethan play texts, including two by Ford, and may represent a pronunciation of 'Say ye'. But 'Why' asks the question which Annabella answers.

16. *I . . . thee*] I did not seek you out, woo you.

19. *case*] state.

20. *would needs be doing*] couldn't wait; with a play on the sense for *doing* of 'copulating'.

23. *for honour*] to save my reputation.

25. *quean*] whore.

29. *stay . . . stomach*] appease your appetite (for information).

I'm content t' acquaint you with: the man,   30
The more than man that got this sprightly boy—
For 'tis a boy, that for your glory, sir,
Your heir shall be a son—
Soranzo.   Damnable monster!
Annabella. Nay, an you will not hear, I'll speak no more.
Soranzo. Yes, speak, and speak thy last.
Annabella.   A match, a match.   35
This noble creature was in every part
So angel-like, so glorious, that a woman
Who had not been but human as was I
Would have kneeled to him and have begged for love.
You? Why, you are not worthy once to name   40
His name without true worship, or indeed,
Unless you kneeled, to hear another name him.
Soranzo. What was he called?
Annabella.   We are not come to that.
Let it suffice that you shall have the glory
To father what so brave a father got.   45
In brief, had not this chance fall'n out as 't doth,
I never had been troubled with a thought
That you had been a creature; but for marriage,
I scarce dream yet of that.
Soranzo. Tell me his name!
Annabella.   Alas, alas, there's all;   50
Will you believe?
Soranzo.   What?
Annabella.   You shall never know.
Soranzo. How!
Annabella.   Never. If you do, let me be cursed.
Soranzo. Not know it, strumpet? I'll rip up thy heart
And find it there.
Annabella.   Do, do.
Soranzo.   And with my teeth

---

34. *an*] if.
35. *match*] bargain.
45. *brave*] handsome, splendid.
48. *been a creature*] been in existence.
48–9. *but for . . . of that*] perhaps: 'as for our really being married, I can still hardly imagine such a thing.'

Tear the prodigious lecher joint by joint.   55
Annabella. Ha, ha, ha! The man's merry.
Soranzo.   Dost thou laugh?
    Come, whore, tell me your lover, or by truth
    I'll hew thy flesh to shreds. Who is 't?
Annabella. (*Sings*) '*Che morte più dolce che morire per amore?*'
Soranzo. Thus will I pull thy hair, and thus I'll drag   60
    Thy lust-belepered body through the dust.
    Yet tell his name.
Annabella. (*Sings*) '*Morendo in gratia a lui, morirei senza*
    dolore.'
Soranzo. Dost thou triumph? The treasure of the earth
    Shall not redeem thee; were there kneeling kings   65
    Did beg thy life, or angels did come down
    To plead in tears, yet should not all prevail
    Against my rage. Dost thou not tremble yet?
Annabella. At what? To die? No. Be a gallant hangman.
    I dare thee to the worst; strike, and strike home;   70
    I leave revenge behind, and thou shalt feel 't.
Soranzo. Yet tell me ere thou diest, and tell me truly:
    Knows thy old father this?
Annabella.   No, by my life.
Soranzo. Wilt thou confess, and I will spare thy life?
Annabella. My life! I will not buy my life so dear.   75
Soranzo. I will not slack my vengeance.
               Enter VASQUES.
Vasques.   What d'ee mean, sir?
Soranzo. Forbear, Vasques. Such a damnèd whore
    Deserves no pity.
Vasques.   Now the gods forfend!
    And would you be her executioner, and kill her in your

---

55. *prodigious*] monstrous.
59.] 'What death is sweeter than to die for love?' Ford found this sentence, and several others used in the play, in John Florio's Italian phrase-book *Florio his First Fruits* (1578).
61. *lust-belepered*] made loathsome by lust, as a leper by his sores.
63.] 'Dying in favour with him, I would die without pain.'
64. *triumph*] stressed on the second syllable.
76. *slack*] (a) forgo; (b) delay.
78. *forfend*] forbid.

rage too? O, 'twere most unmanlike! She is your wife;   80
what faults hath been done by her before she married you
were not against you. Alas, poor lady, what hath she
committed, which any lady in Italy in the like case would
not? Sir, you must be ruled by your reason and not by
your fury; that were unhuman and beastly.   85
Soranzo. She shall not live.
Vasques. Come, she must. You would have her confess the
authors of her present misfortunes, I warrant 'ee; 'tis an
unconscionable demand, and she should lose the estima-
tion that I, for my part, hold of her worth, if she had done   90
it. Why, sir, you ought not of all men living to know it.
Good sir, be reconciled. Alas, good gentlewoman!
Annabella. Pish, do not beg for me. I prize my life
As nothing; if the man will needs be mad,
Why let him take it.
Soranzo.   Vasques, hear'st thou this?   95
Vasques. Yes, and commend her for it: in this she shows the
nobleness of a gallant spirit, and beshrew my heart but it
becomes her rarely. [*Aside to Soranzo*] Sir, in any case
smother your revenge; leave the scenting-out your
wrongs to me; be ruled, as you respect your honour, or   100
you mar all. [*Aloud*.] Sir, if ever my service were of any
credit with you, be not so violent in your distractions.
You are married now; what a triumph might the report of
this give to other neglected suitors! 'Tis as manlike to
bear extremities as godlike to forgive.   105
Soranzo. O Vasques, Vasques, in this piece of flesh,
This faithless face of hers, had I laid up
The treasure of my heart!—Hadst thou been virtuous,
Fair, wicked woman, not the matchless joys
Of life itself had made me wish to live   110

---

88. *authors*] persons responsible. (Vasques's use of the plural may insinu-
ate that Annabella must have had accomplices, or that she had more lovers
than one.)

97. *beshrew*] curse.

101–2. *were . . . credit*] deserved any reward.

107–8. *laid . . . heart*] invested my hopes and feelings. The phrasing echoes
Jesus's teaching that people should lay up their treasure in heaven, not on
earth (Matthew vi.19–21).

110. *life*] heaven.

With any saint but thee. Deceitful creature,
How hast thou mocked my hopes, and in the shame
Of thy lewd womb even buried me alive!
I did too dearly love thee.
Vasques.   This is well.
   (*Aside* [*to him*]) Follow this temper with some passion; be   115
   brief and moving; 'tis for the purpose.
Soranzo. [*To Annabella*] Be witness to my words thy soul
        and thoughts,
   And tell me, didst not think that in my heart
   I did too superstitiously adore thee?
Annabella. I must confess, I know you loved me well.   120
Soranzo. And wouldst thou use me thus? O Annabella,
   Be thou assured, whatsoe'er the villain was
   That thus hath tempted thee to this disgrace,
   Well he might lust, but never loved like me.
   He doted on the picture that hung out   125
   Upon thy cheeks, to please his humorous eye,
   Not on the part I loved, which was thy heart,
   And, as I thought, thy virtues.
Annabella.   O my lord!
   These words wound deeper than your sword could do.
Vasques. Let me not ever take comfort, but I begin to weep   130
   myself, so much I pity him. Why, madam, I knew when
   his rage was overpassed what it would come to.
Soranzo. Forgive me, Annabella. Though thy youth
   Hath tempted thee above thy strength to folly,
   Yet will not I forget what I should be,   135
   And what I am, a husband; in that name
   Is hid divinity. If I do find
   That thou wilt yet be true, here I remit
   All former faults, and take thee to my bosom.
Vasques. By my troth, and that's a point of noble charity.   140

---

115. *temper*] calmness.
   passion] outburst of feeling.
119. *too superstitiously adore*] idolise.
126. *humorous*] capricious.
138. *remit*] forgive.
140. *point*] example.

Annabella. Sir, on my knees—
Soranzo.   Rise up; you shall not kneel.
Get you to your chamber, see you make no show
Of alteration; I'll be with you straight.
My reason tells me now that 'tis as common
To err in frailty as to be a woman.   145
Go to your chamber.   *Exit* ANNABELLA.
Vasques. So, this was somewhat to the matter. What do you
think of your heaven of happiness now, sir?
Soranzo. I carry hell about me! All my blood
Is fired in swift revenge.   150
Vasques. That may be, but know you how, or on whom? Alas,
to marry a great woman, being made great in the stock to
your hand, is a usual sport in these days; but to know
what ferret it was that haunted your cony-berry—there's
the cunning.   155
Soranzo. I'll make her tell herself, or—
Vasques. Or what? You must not do so. Let me yet persuade
your sufferance a little while. Go to her, use her mildly;
win her if it be possible to a voluntary, to a weeping tune;
for the rest, if all hit, I will not miss my mark. Pray, sir, go   160
in; the next news I tell you shall be wonders.
Soranzo. Delay in vengeance gives a heavier blow.   *Exit.*
Vasques. [*To himself*] Ah, sirrah, here's work for the nonce! I
had a suspicion of a bad matter in my head a pretty whiles
ago; but after my madam's scurvy looks here at home, her   165

142–3. *see . . . alteration*] take care not to appear ill or distressed.

147. *matter*] purpose.

152.] A chain of puns. *great*] (a) of high rank; (b) great with child. *stock*]
(a) butt or handle; (b) body; (c) rabbit-burrow.

152–3. *to your hand*] all ready for you.

154. *haunted your cony-berry*] frequented your rabbit-burrow. (Land was
set aside for rabbits to breed in, and when meat or sport was needed they
were hunted by muzzled ferrets; the ferret of the metaphor may be wild, or
belong to a poacher.)

cony] (a) rabbit; (b) slang for the female sexual organ.

155. *cunning*] skill.

158. *sufferance*] patience.

159. *voluntary*] (a) piece of music played or sung at the performer's choice;
(b) oath or other statement made of free will.

160. *if all hit*] if everything goes right.

163. *nonce*] present occasion.

waspish perverseness and loud fault-finding, then I remembered the proverb, that where hens crow and cocks
hold their peace there are sorry houses. 'Sfoot, if the
lower parts of a she-tailor's cunning can cover such a
swelling in the stomach, I'll never blame a false stitch in   170
a shoe whiles I live again. Up, and up so quick? And so
quickly too? 'Twere a fine policy to learn by whom; this
must be known. And I have thought on 't—here's the
way, or none.

Enter PUTANA.

What, crying, old mistress? Alas, alas, I cannot blame 'ee.   175
We have a lord, heaven help us, is so mad as the devil
himself, the more shame for him.

Putana. O Vasques, that ever I was born to see this day! Doth
   he use thee so too sometimes, Vasques?

Vasques. Me! Why, he makes a dog of me; but if some were of   180
   my mind, I know what we would do. As sure as I am an
   honest man, he will go near to kill my lady with unkind-
   ness. Say she be with child, is that such a matter for a
   young woman of her years to be blamed for?

Putana. Alas, good heart, it is against her will full sore.   185

Vasques. I durst be sworn, all his madness is for that she will
   not confess whose 'tis; which he will know, and when he
   doth know it, I am so well acquainted with his humour
   that he will forget all straight. Well I could wish she
   would in plain terms tell all, for that's the way indeed.   190

Putana. Do you think so?

Vasques. Foh, I know 't; provided that he did not win her to
   't by force. He was once in a mind that you could tell, and
   meant to have wrung it out of you, but I somewhat
   pacified him for that; yet sure you know a great deal.   195

Putana. Heaven forgive us all, I know a little, Vasques.

---

169. *lower . . . cunning*] elements of a dressmaker's skill (with a bawdy play
in *lower parts*).

171. *Up*] risen up, inflated, i.e. pregnant.

quick] alive.

172. *policy*] piece of craft.

176. *mad*] furious.

188. *humour*] turn of mind.

Vasques. Why should you not? Who else should? Upon my
conscience, she loves you dearly, and you would not
betray her to any affliction for the world.

Putana. Not for all the world, by my faith and troth, Vasques.   200

Vasques. 'Twere pity of your life if you should; but in this you
should both relieve her present discomforts, pacify my
lord, and gain yourself everlasting love and preferment.

Putana. Dost think so, Vasques?

Vasques. Nay, I know 't. Sure 'twas some near and entire   205
friend.

Putana. 'Twas a dear friend indeed; but—

Vasques. But what? Fear not to name him; my life between
you and danger. Faith, I think 'twas no base fellow.

Putana. Thou wilt stand between me and harm?   210

Vasques. Ud's pity, what else? You shall be rewarded too;
trust me.

Putana. 'Twas even no worse than her own brother.

Vasques. Her brother Giovanni, I warrant 'ee!

Putana. Even he, Vasques; as brave a gentleman as ever   215
kissed fair lady. O, they love most perpetually.

Vasques. A brave gentleman indeed; why, therein I commend
her choice. [*Aside*] Better and better. [*To her*] You are
sure 'twas he?

Putana. Sure; and you shall see he will not be long from her   220
too.

Vasques. He were to blame if he would. But may I believe
thee?

Putana. Believe me! Why, dost think I am a Turk or a Jew?
No, Vasques, I have known their dealings too long to   225
belie them now.

Vasques. [*Calling out*] Where are you? There within, sirs!

Enter Banditti.

Putana. How now, what are these?

---

205. *entire*] (a) devoted; (b) (of animals) not castrated.
207. *dear*] (a) well-loved; (b) costly.
211. *Ud's*] God's.
215. *brave*] fine, handsome.
226. *belie*] tell lies about.

Vasques. You shall know presently. Come, sirs, take me this
    old damnable hag, gag her instantly, and put out her eyes.   230
    Quickly, quickly!   [*They seize her.*]
Putana. Vasques, Vasques!
Vasques. Gag her I say. 'Sfoot, d'ee suffer her to prate? What
    d'ee fumble about? Let me come to her. I'll help your old
    gums, you toad-bellied bitch! [*He gags* PUTANA.] Sirs,   235
    carry her closely into the coal-house and put out her eyes
    instantly. If she roars, slit her nose; d'ee hear, be speedy
    and sure.

                        Exeunt [Banditti] *with* PUTANA.
    Why, this is excellent and above expectation. Her own
    brother? O, horrible! To what a height of liberty in dam-   240
    nation hath the devil trained our age! Her brother, well!
    There's yet but a beginning. I must to my lord, and tutor
    him better in his points of vengeance. Now I see how a
    smooth tale goes beyond a smooth tail. But soft, what
    thing comes next?   245

                  Enter GIOVANNI.

    Giovanni! As I would wish. My belief is strengthened; 'tis
    as firm as winter and summer.
Giovanni. Where's my sister?
Vasques. Troubled with a new sickness, my lord; she's some-
    what ill.   250
Giovanni. Took too much of the flesh, I believe.
Vasques. Troth, sir, and you I think have e'en hit it; but my
    virtuous lady—
Giovanni. Where's she?   [*Gives him money.*]
Vasques. In her chamber; please you visit her? She is alone.   255

---

229. *presently*] right away.

233. *prate*] prattle.

236. *closely*] secretly.

240–1. *liberty in damnation*] freedom in committing damnable sins.

241. *trained*] (a) enticed; (b) educated.

244. *goes beyond*] outwits, 'gets round'.

    smooth tail] figurative for 'woman'. Vasques congratulates himself on the
success of his own smooth tale.

247. *as firm . . . summer*] as certain as the regular cycle of the seasons.

251. *Took . . . flesh*] (a) ate too much meat; (b) had too much sex (a sense
obviously unintended by Giovanni).

Your liberality hath doubly made me your servant, and
ever shall, ever—   *Exit* GIOVANNI.

Enter SORANZO.

Sir, I am made a man; I have plied my cue with cunning
and success. I beseech you, let's be private.

Soranzo. My lady's brother's come, now he'll know all.   260

Vasques. Let him know 't. I have made some of them fast
enough. How have you dealt with my lady?

Soranzo. Gently, as thou hast counselled. O, my soul
Runs circular in sorrow for revenge!
But Vasques, thou shalt know—   265

Vasques. Nay, I will know no more, for now comes your turn
to know; I would not talk so openly with you. Let my
young master take time enough, and go at pleasure; he is
sold to death, and the devil shall not ransom him. Sir, I
beseech you, your privacy.   270

Soranzo. No conquest can gain glory of my fear.   *Exeunt.*

---

256. *liberality*] (a) generosity; (b) sexual libertinism.

258. *made a man*] perhaps a misprint for 'a made man', one whose success
is certain.

plied my cue] played my part.

267–8 *my young master*] Giovanni (with ironical deference).

271.] probably 'Whatever defeats I may suffer, my enemy shall not have
the glory of seeing me show fear.'

Act V

[v. i]

Enter ANNABELLA *above.*

Annabella. Pleasures, farewell, and all ye thriftless minutes
    Wherein false joys have spun a weary life!
    To these my fortunes now I take my leave.
    Thou precious Time, that swiftly rid'st in post
    Over the world, to finish up the race   5
    Of my last fate; here stay thy restless course,
    And bear to ages that are yet unborn
    A wretched woeful woman's tragedy.
    My conscience now stands up against my lust
    With depositions charactered in guilt,   10

Enter Friar.

    And tells me I am lost. Now I confess,
    Beauty that clothes the outside of the face
    Is cursèd if it be not clothed with grace.
    Here like a turtle, mewed up in a cage
    Unmated, I converse with air and walls,   15
    And descant on my vile unhappiness.
    O Giovanni, that hast had the spoil

V.i.o.1.S.D. *above*] on the upper stage, as on her balcony or at a window.
4. *in post*] at full speed.
9. *against*] to bear witness against.
10. *depositions*] written testimony.
charactered] lettered.
guilt] with a pun on 'gilt', i.e. lettered in gold to demand special attention.
10.1.S.D. The Friar enters below.
14. *turtle*] turtle-dove.
mewed] cooped.
15. *Unmated*] The turtle-dove was proverbially devoted to its mate.
16. *descant on*] (a) sing about; (b) complain of.
17–18. *had . . . Of*] (a) plundered; (b) destroyed.

Of thine own virtues and my modest fame,
Would thou hadst been less subject to those stars
That luckless reigned at my nativity!   20
O, would the scourge due to my black offence
Might pass from thee, that I alone might feel
The torment of an uncontrollèd flame!

Friar. [*Aside*] What's this I hear?

Annabella.   That man, that blessèd friar,
Who joined in ceremonial knot my hand   25
To him whose wife I now am, told me oft
I trod the path to death, and showed me how.
But they who sleep in lethargies of lust
Hug their confusion, making heaven unjust,
And so did I.

Friar. [*Aside*]   Here's music to the soul!   30

Annabella. Forgive me, my good genius, and this once
Be helpful to my ends! Let some good man
Pass this way, to whose trust I may commit
This paper double-lined with tears and blood;
Which being granted, here I sadly vow   35
Repentance, and a leaving of that life
I long have died in.

Friar.   Lady, heaven hath heard you,
And hath by providence ordained that I
Should be his minister for your behoof.

Annabella. Ha, what are you?

Friar.   Your brother's friend the friar;   40
Glad in my soul that I have lived to hear
This free confession 'twixt your peace and you.
What would you, or to whom? Fear not to speak.

---

23. *uncontrollèd flame*] (a) of passion; (b) of hell-fire.

28. *lethargies of lust*] moral torpor induced by lust.

29. *Hug their confusion*] embrace their own damnation.

making heaven unjust] i.e. 'deceiving themselves into thinking that God will not deal justly with them'; or perhaps 'blaming heaven for the follies they commit'.

31. *good genius*] protecting spirit, guardian angel.

34. *double-lined . . . blood*] written in blood and interlined with tears.

35. *sadly*] (a) soberly; (b) sorrowfully.

37. *died*] i.e. died spiritually.

39. *behoof*] advantage.

Annabella. Is heaven so bountiful? Then I have found
    More favour than I hoped. Here, holy man: 45
                        Throws a letter.
    Commend me to my brother; give him that,
    That letter; bid him read it and repent.
    Tell him that I—imprisoned in my chamber,
    Barred of all company, even of my guardian,
    Who gives me cause of much suspect—have time   50
    To blush at what hath passed; bid him be wise,
    And not believe the friendship of my lord.
    I fear much more than I can speak. Good father,
    The place is dangerous, and spies are busy.
    I must break off. You'll do 't?
Friar.   Be sure I will,   55
    And fly with speed. My blessing ever rest
    With thee, my daughter; live to die more blest!   *Exit.*
Annabella. Thanks to the heavens, who have prolonged my
    breath
    To this good use. Now I can welcome death.   *Exit.*

[v. ii]

Enter SORANZO *and* VASQUES.

Vasques. Am I to be believed now? First, marry a strumpet
    that cast herself away upon you but to laugh at your
    horns? To feast on your disgrace, riot in your vexations,
    cuckold you in your bride-bed, waste your estate upon
    panders and bawds?   5
Soranzo. No more, I say, no more!
Vasques. A cuckold is a goodly tame beast, my lord.
Soranzo. I am resolved; urge not another word.
    My thoughts are great, and all as resolute
    As thunder. In mean time I'll cause our lady   10
    To deck herself in all her bridal robes,

---

    50. *Who*] which.
suspect] suspicion, fear.

    V.ii.2–3. *your horns*] It was a traditional joke that horns grew invisibly from
the forehead of a cuckold.
    3. *riot in*] delight in.

Kiss her, and fold her gently in my arms.
Begone. Yet hear you, are the banditti ready
To wait in ambush?

Vasques. Good sir, trouble not yourself about other business   15
than your own resolution. Remember that time lost cannot be recalled.

Soranzo. With all the cunning words thou canst, invite
The states of Parma to my birthday's feast;
Haste to my brother rival and his father;   20
Entreat them gently, bid them not to fail.
Be speedy and return.

Vasques. Let not your pity betray you till my coming back;
think upon incest and cuckoldry.

Soranzo. Revenge is all the ambition I aspire;   25
To that I'll climb or fall. My blood's on fire.   *Exeunt.*

[v. iii]

Enter GIOVANNI.

Giovanni. Busy opinion is an idle fool,
That, as a school-rod keeps a child in awe,
Frights the unexperienced temper of the mind.
So did it me, who, ere my precious sister
Was married, thought all taste of love would die   5
In such a contract; but I find no change
Of pleasure in this formal law of sports.
She is still one to me, and every kiss
As sweet and as delicious as the first
I reaped, when yet the privilege of youth   10
Entitled her a virgin. O, the glory
Of two united hearts like hers and mine!
Let poring book-men dream of other worlds;
My world, and all of happiness, is here,
And I'd not change it for the best to come.   15

---

19. *states*] persons of high rank or office.
25. *aspire*] ardently desire.

V.iii.1. *Busy opinion*] meddlesome common opinion.
idle] futile.
7. *in . . . sports*] resulting from these conventional rules of the game.

A life of pleasure is Elysium.

Enter Friar.

Father, you enter on the jubilee
Of my retired delights. Now I can tell you
The hell you oft have prompted is nought else
But slavish and fond superstitious fear;   20
And I could prove it, too—
Friar.   Thy blindness slays thee;
Look there, 'tis writ to thee.   *Gives the letter.*
Giovanni. From whom?
Friar. Unrip the seals and see;
The blood's yet seething hot, that will anon   25
Be frozen harder than congealèd coral.
Why d'ee change colour, son?
Giovanni.   'Fore heaven, you make
Some petty devil factor 'twixt my love
And your religion-maskèd sorceries.
Where had you this?
Friar.   Thy conscience, youth, is seared,   30
Else thou wouldst stoop to warning.
Giovanni.   'Tis her hand,
I know 't; and 'tis all written in her blood.
She writes I know not what—death? I'll not fear
An armèd thunderbolt aimed at my heart.
She writes we are discovered—pox on dreams   35
Of low faint-hearted cowardice! Discovered?
The devil we are! Which way is 't possible?
Are we grown traitors to our own delights?

---

16. *Elysium*] the dwelling-place of blest souls after death.

17. *on the jubilee*] at the height. (A jubilee is a time of celebration, usually an anniversary.)

18. *retired*] secluded, private.

19. *prompted*] urged me to think about.

20. *fond*] foolish.

26. *congealèd coral*] Coral was believed to be an underwater plant which hardened when exposed to air.

28. *factor*] intermediary.

30. *seared*] made incapable of feeling, as by being cauterised.

31. *stoop to*] submit to (perhaps with a metaphor of the trained hawk coming under control by 'stooping' to the falconer's 'lure').

Confusion take such dotage, 'tis but forged!
This is your peevish chattering, weak old man.   40

Enter VASQUES.

Now, sir, what news bring you?

Vasques. My lord, according to his yearly custom keeping this
     day a feast in honour of his birthday, by me invites you
     thither; your worthy father, with the Pope's reverend
     nuncio and other magnificoes of Parma, have promised   45
     their presence. Will 't please you to be of the number?

Giovanni. Yes, tell them I dare come.

Vasques. Dare come?

Giovanni. So I said; and tell him more, I will come.

Vasques. These words are strange to me.   50

Giovanni. Say I will come.

Vasques. You will not miss?

Giovanni. Yet more? I'll come! Sir, are you answered?

Vasques. So I'll say. My service to you.   *Exit.*

Friar. You will not go, I trust.

Giovanni.   Not go! For what?   55

Friar. O, do not go! This feast, I'll gage my life,
     Is but a plot to train you to your ruin;
     Be ruled, you sha' not go.

Giovanni.   Not go? Stood Death
     Threat'ning his armies of confounding plagues,
     With hosts of dangers hot as blazing stars,   60
     I would be there. Not go? Yes, and resolve
     To strike as deep in slaughter as they all,
     For I will go.

Friar.   Go where thou wilt; I see
     The wildness of thy fate draws to an end,
     To a bad, fearful end. I must not stay   65
     To know thy fall; back to Bononia I

---

39. *dotage*] nonsense.
40. *peevish*] (a) senseless; (b) spiteful.
52. *miss*] fail.
56. *gage*] wager.
57. *train*] entice.
60. *blazing stars*] comets, believed to be ominous.

With speed will haste, and shun this coming blow.
Parma, farewell; would I had never known thee,
Or aught of thine! Well, youngman, since no prayer
Can make thee safe, I leave thee to despair.   *Exit.*   70
Giovanni. Despair, or tortures of a thousand hells,
    All's one to me: I have set up my rest.
    Now, now, work serious thoughts on baneful plots;
    Be all a man, my soul; let not the curse
    Of old prescription rend from me the gall   75
    Of courage, which enrols a glorious death.
    If I must totter like a well-grown oak,
    Some under-shrubs shall in my weighty fall
    Be crushed to splits; with me they all shall perish.

                                  Exit.

[v. iv]

Enter SORANZO, VASQUES *and* Banditti.

Soranzo. You will not fail, or shrink in the attempt?
Vasques. I will undertake for their parts.—Be sure, my mas-
    ters, to be bloody enough, and as unmerciful as if you
    were preying upon a rich booty on the very mountains of
    Liguria. For your pardons, trust to my lord; but for   5
    reward you shall trust none but your own pockets.
Banditti omnes. We'll make a murder.
Soranzo. Here's gold, here's more; want nothing. What you
      do
    Is noble, and an act of brave revenge.

---

69. *youngman*] in use as a single word, probably stressed on the first syllable.

72. *set up my rest*] committed my last stakes (in the card game primero, like betting one's last chips at poker).

73. *baneful*] life-destroying, poisonous.

75. *prescription*] custom.

gall] (a) organ producing anger or fierceness; (b) growth upon oak-trees, used for making ink and hence in records (see 76 below).

76. *enrols*] honourably records.

79. *splits*] splinters.

V.iv.2. *undertake for*] vouch for.

5. *Liguria*] a region whose mountains run between Parma and Genoa.

I'll make ye rich, banditti, and all free.   10

Banditti omnes. Liberty! Liberty!

Vasques. Hold, take every man a vizard. When ye are withdrawn, keep as much silence as you can possibly. You know the watchword, till which be spoken, move not, but when you hear that, rush in like a stormy flood. I need not   15
instruct ye in your own profession.

Banditti omnes. No, no, no.

Vasques. In, then; your ends are profit and preferment. Away!
    Exeunt Banditti.

Soranzo. The guests will all come, Vasques?

Vasques. Yes, sir, and now let me a little edge your resolution: 20
you see nothing is unready to this great work but a great mind in you. Call to your remembrance your disgraces, your loss of honour, Hippolita's blood, and arm your courage in your own wrongs; so shall you best right those wrongs in vengeance which you may truly call your own.   25

Soranzo. 'Tis well; the less I speak, the more I burn,
And blood shall quench that flame.

Vasques. Now you begin to turn Italian! This beside: when my young incest-monger comes, he will be sharp set on his old bit. Give him time enough; let him have your cham-   30
ber and bed at liberty; let my hot hare have law ere he be hunted to his death, that if it be possible he may post to hell in the very act of his damnation.

Enter GIOVANNI.

Soranzo. It shall be so; and see, as we would wish,
He comes himself first.—Welcome, my much-loved
brother!   35

---

10. *free*] The Banditti are outlaws; Soranzo promises to restore their civil rights and liberties.

12. *vizard*] mask.

20. *edge*] sharpen.

29. *sharp set*] keen, eager for food or (as here) sex.

30. *bit*] morsel of food; tempting girl.

31. *hot hare*] taken to represent excessive and unnatural sexual activity.

law] a start, as required by the rules of hunting; time to get going.

32. *post*] speed.

33. *in . . . damnation*] The idea of a revenge that would destroy soul as well as body was familiar in Jacobean drama, e.g. in *Hamlet*, III.iii.73–95.

35. *brother*] brother-in-law.

Now I perceive you honour me; y' are welcome.
But where's my father?
Giovanni.　　　　　　　　With the other states,
　　Attending on the nuncio of the Pope
　　To wait upon him hither. How's my sister?
Soranzo. Like a good housewife, scarcely ready yet;　　40
　　Y' are best walk to her chamber.
Giovanni.　　　　　　　　If you will.
Soranzo. I must expect my honourable friends;
　　Good brother, get her forth.
Giovanni.　　　　　　　You are busy, sir.　　*Exit.*
Vasques. Even as the great devil himself would have it! Let
　　him go and glut himself in his own destruction.　　45
　　　　　　　　　　　　　　　　　Flourish.
　　Hark, the nuncio is at hand. Good sir, be ready to receive
　　him.

　　　　Enter Cardinal, FLORIO, DONADO, RICHARDETTO
　　　　　　　　　　and Attendants.

Soranzo. Most reverend lord, this grace hath made me proud
　　That you vouchsafe my house; I ever rest
　　Your humble servant for this noble favour.　　50
Cardinal. You are our friend, my lord; his Holiness
　　Shall understand how zealously you honour
　　Saint Peter's vicar in his substitute.
　　Our special love to you.
Soranzo.　　　　　　　Signiors, to you
　　My welcome, and my ever best of thanks　　55
　　For this so memorable courtesy.
　　Pleaseth your grace to walk near?
Cardinal.　　　　　　　　My lord, we come
　　To celebrate your feast with civil mirth,

---

37. *father*] father-in-law.
states] dignitaries, as at V.ii.19.
39. *wait upon*] attend.
42. *expect*] wait for.
48. *grace*] honour.
49. *vouchsafe*] confer upon.
53. *Saint Peter's vicar*] the Pope, whom the nuncio represents.
57. *Pleaseth your grace*] may it please your grace.
58. *civil mirth*] well-behaved merry-making.

As ancient custom teacheth; we will go.

Soranzo. Attend his grace, there!—Signiors, keep your way.   60

                                        Exeunt.

[v. v]

      Enter GIOVANNI *and* ANNABELLA *lying on a bed.*

Giovanni. What, changed so soon? Hath your new sprightly
    lord
    Found out a trick in night-games more than we
    Could know in our simplicity? Ha, is 't so?
    Or does the fit come on you, to prove treacherous
    To your past vows and oaths?
Annabella.   Why should you jest   5
    At my calamity, without all sense
    Of the approaching dangers you are in?
Giovanni. What danger's half so great as thy revolt?
    Thou art a faithless sister, else thou know'st
    Malice, or any treachery beside,   10
    Would stoop to my bent brows. Why, I hold fate
    Clasped in my fist, and could command the course
    Of time's eternal motion, hadst thou been
    One thought more steady than an ebbing sea.
    And what? You'll now be honest, that's resolved?   15
Annabella. Brother, dear brother, know what I have been,
    And know that now there's but a dining-time
    'Twixt us and our confusion. Let's not waste
    These precious hours in vain and useless speech.
    Alas, these gay attires were not put on   20

---

60. *keep your way*] walk straight ahead.

V.v.0.1.S.D]. Some contemporary plays call for a bed to be 'thrust out' on the stage with a person in it, as may have happened here. Alternatively, the lovers may have been disclosed on a bed within the discovery space back-stage, coming forward once the location is established.

4. *fit*] capricious impulse.

11. *stoop . . . brows*] yield to my frown.

15. *honest*] chaste.

17. *but a dining-time*] only long enough to eat a dinner. (Uncorrected copies of the quarto read 'a dying time'.)

18. *confusion*] destruction.

But to some end; this sudden solemn feast
Was not ordained to riot in expense.
I that have now been chambered here alone,
Barred of my guardian, or of any else,
Am not for nothing at an instant freed   25
To fresh access. Be not deceived, my brother:
This banquet is an harbinger of death
To you and me; resolve yourself it is,
And be prepared to welcome it.
Giovanni.   Well, then,
The schoolmen teach that all this globe of earth   30
Shall be consumed to ashes in a minute.
Annabella. So I have read too.
Giovanni.   But 'twere somewhat strange
To see the waters burn. Could I believe
This might be true, I could believe as well
There might be hell or heaven.
Annabella.   That's most certain.   35
Giovanni. A dream, a dream; else in this other world
We should know one another.
Annabella.   So we shall.
Giovanni. Have you heard so?
Annabella.   For certain.
Giovanni.   But d'ee think
That I shall see you there, you look on me;
May we kiss one another, prate or laugh,   40
Or do as we do here?
Annabella.   I know not that.
But good, for the present, what d'ee mean

---

21. *solemn*] ceremonious, sumptuous.

22. *to . . . expense*] merely for the sake of squandering money.

25–6. *freed . . . access*] allowed to see visitors again.

28. *resolve yourself*] assure yourself.

30. *schoolmen*] mediaeval theologians.

30–1. *this globe . . . minute*] The problem of interpreting some passages in Revelation xx–xxi goes back at least to St Augustine.

39. *you look on me*] and that you will see me there.

40. *prate*] talk idly.

41. *do as we do here*] with the specific sense of 'make love' as well as the more general sense.

42. *good*] a term of address, like 'sweet', 'dear'.

> To free yourself from danger? Some way, think
> How to escape; I'm sure the guests are come.

Giovanni. Look up, look here; what see you in my face?   45

Annabella. Distraction and a troubled countenance.

Giovanni. Death, and a swift repining wrath—yet look,
> What see you in mine eyes?

Annabella.   Methinks you weep.

Giovanni. I do indeed. These are the funeral tears
> Shed on your grave; these furrowed up my cheeks   50
> When first I loved and knew not how to woo.
> Fair Annabella, should I here repeat
> The story of my life, we might lose time.
> Be record all the spirits of the air,
> And all things else that are, that day and night,   55
> Early and late, the tribute which my heart
> Hath paid to Annabella's sacred love
> Hath been these tears, which are her mourners now.
> Never till now did Nature do her best
> To show a matchless beauty to the world,   60
> Which in an instant, ere it scarce was seen,
> The jealous Destinies required again.
> Pray, Annabella, pray; since we must part,
> Go thou white in thy soul, to fill a throne
> Of innocence and sanctity in heaven.   65
> Pray, pray, my sister.

Annabella.   Then I see your drift.
> Ye blessèd angels, guard me!

Giovanni.   So say I.
> Kiss me. If ever after-times should hear
> Of our fast-knit affections, though perhaps
> The laws of conscience and of civil use   70

---

46. *Distraction*] mental disturbance, temporary madness.

47. *repining*] angry.

54. *spirits of the air*] Such spirits, not necessarily evil in pagan and Neoplatonic thought, approximated to devils in orthodox Christian belief and were thought likely to be present at an act like the one now planned.

64. *white in thy soul*] not the orthodox view, but Neoplatonists taught that the soul cannot be defiled by the sins of the body.

66. *drift*] intention.

70. *civil use*] civilised custom.

May justly blame us, yet when they but know
Our loves, that love will wipe away that rigour
Which would in other incests be abhorred.
Give me your hand. How sweetly life doth run
In these well-coloured veins! How constantly   75
These palms do promise health! But I could chide
With Nature for this cunning flattery.
Kiss me again—forgive me.
Annabella.   With my heart.
Giovanni. Farewell.
Annabella.   Will you be gone?
Giovanni.   Be dark, bright sun,
And make this midday night, that thy gilt rays   80
May not behold a deed will turn their splendour
More sooty than the poets feign their Styx!
One other kiss, my sister.
Annabella.   What means this?
Giovanni. To save thy fame, and kill thee in a kiss.

                                        Stabs her.

Thus die, and die by me, and by my hand.   85
Revenge is mine; honour doth love command.
Annabella. O brother, by your hand?
Giovanni.   When thou art dead
I'll give my reasons for 't; for to dispute
With thy—even in thy death—most lovely beauty
Would make me stagger to perform this act   90
Which I most glory in.
Annabella. Forgive him, heaven—and me my sins. Farewell,
Brother, unkind, unkind—mercy, great heaven!—O—O!

                                        Dies.

---

72. *wipe . . . rigour*] remove the shame of that violence of passion.

75. *constantly*] confidently.

78. *forgive me*] Like an executioner (see V.vi.33), Giovanni asks pardon of
his victim.

82. *Styx*] in Greek mythology, a black poisonous river flowing round the
underworld.

86. *Revenge is mine*] But see Romans xii.19, 'Vengeance is mine; I will
repay, saith the Lord', famously quoted by Hieronimo in Kyd's *The Spanish
Tragedy*, III.xiii.1.

90. *stagger to perform*] hesitate in performing.

93. *unkind*] with the contemporary implication of 'unnatural'.

Giovanni. She's dead. Alas, good soul! The hapless fruit
    That in her womb received its life from me   95
    Hath had from me a cradle and a grave.
    I must not dally. This sad marriage-bed,
    In all her best, bore her alive and dead.
    Soranzo, thou hast missed thy aim in this;
    I have prevented now thy reaching plots,   100
    And killed a love, for whose each drop of blood
    I would have pawned my heart. Fair Annabella,
    How over-glorious art thou in thy wounds,
    Triumphing over infamy and hate!
    Shrink not, courageous hand; stand up, my heart,   105
    And boldly act my last and greater part!

                              Exit with the body.

[v. vi]

    A banquet. Enter Cardinal, FLORIO, DONADO, SORANZO,
RICHARDETTO, VASQUES *and* Attendants; *they take their places.*

Vasques. [*Aside to Soranzo*] Remember, sir, what you have to
    do; be wise and resolute.
Soranzo. [*Aside to Vasques*] Enough, my heart is fixed. [*To
    Cardinal*] Pleaseth your grace
    To taste these coarse confections? Though the use
    Of such set entertainments more consists   5
    In custom than in cause, yet, reverend sir,
    I am still made your servant by your presence.

---

    98. *In all her best*] (a) at her highest point; (b) in her best array (her wedding-dress; see V.ii.11).

    100. *prevented*] forestalled.

    reaching] far-reaching.

    102. *pawned*] pledged, put at risk.

    103. *over-glorious*] beautiful beyond measure.

    V.vi.0.1.S.D. A banquet] Stage time makes it possible for V.v to take place while Soranzo and his guests process into the dining-room, where they are now about to eat.

    4. *coarse confections*] homely dishes.

    4–6. *Though . . . cause*] 'although such formal entertainments are held more for the sake of keeping up a custom than for any real benefit'.

    7. *made your servant by*] i.e. indebted to you for.

Cardinal. And we your friend.
Soranzo. But where's my brother Giovanni?

Enter GIOVANNI *with a heart upon his dagger.*

Giovanni. Here, here, Soranzo! Trimmed in reeking blood   10
    That triumphs over death; proud in the spoil
    Of love and vengeance! Fate, or all the powers
    That guide the motions of immortal souls,
    Could not prevent me.
Cardinal.   What means this?
Florio. Son Giovanni!
Soranzo. [*Aside*]   Shall I be forestalled?   15
Giovanni. Be not amazed. If your misgiving hearts
    Shrink at an idle sight, what bloodless fear
    Of coward passion would have seized your senses,
    Had you beheld the rape of life and beauty
    Which I have acted? My sister, O my sister!   20
Florio. Ha! What of her?
Giovanni.   The glory of my deed
    Darkened the midday sun, made noon as night.
    You came to feast, my lords, with dainty fare;
    I came to feast too, but I digged for food
    In a much richer mine than gold or stone   25
    Of any value balanced. 'Tis a heart,
    A heart, my lords, in which is mine entombed.
    Look well upon 't; d'ee know 't?
Vasques. What strange riddle's this?
Giovanni. 'Tis Annabella's heart, 'tis. Why d'ee startle?   30
    I vow 'tis hers. This dagger's point ploughed up

9.] Oddly, Soranzo has not asked about Annabella, who should have been presiding.

10. *Trimmed*] decorated.

reeking] steaming.

11. *spoil*] both 'destruction' and 'plunder'.

16. *misgiving*] apprehensive.

17. *idle sight*] mere spectacle.

26. *balanced*] rated after weighing.

30. *startle*] start, take fright.

31–2. *ploughed . . . womb*] a perversion of a common metaphor for fertile sexuality; and Giovanni's operations are a perverted counterpart of the delivery of a child.

Her fruitful womb, and left to me the fame
Of a most glorious executioner.

Florio. Why, madman, art thyself?

Giovanni. Yes, father, and that times to come may know   35
How as my fate I honoured my revenge,
List, father; to your ears I will yield up
How much I have deserved to be your son.

Florio. What is 't thou say'st?

Giovanni.   Nine moons have had their changes,
Since I first throughly viewed and truly loved   40
Your daughter and my sister.

Florio.   How! Alas,
My lords, he's a frantic madman!

Giovanni.   Father, no.
For nine months' space, in secret I enjoyed
Sweet Annabella's sheets; nine months I lived
A happy monarch of her heart and her.   45
Soranzo, thou know'st this; thy paler cheek
Bears the confounding print of thy disgrace,
For her too fruitful womb too soon bewrayed
The happy passage of our stol'n delights,
And made her mother to a child unborn.   50

Cardinal. Incestuous villain!

Florio.   O, his rage belies him!

Giovanni. It does not, 'tis the oracle of truth;
I vow it is so.

Soranzo.   I shall burst with fury;
Bring the strumpet forth!

Vasques. I shall, sir.   *Exit.*

Giovanni.   Do, sir. Have you all no faith   55
To credit yet my triumphs? Here I swear
By all that you call sacred, by the love

---

33. *glorious*] splendid; famous; triumphant.
34. *art thyself?*] i.e. are you in your right mind?
38.] not only by birth, but as husband to Florio's daughter ('son' was often used for 'son-in-law').
40. *throughly*] thoroughly.
47. *confounding*] shaming.
48. *bewrayed*] revealed.
51. *rage*] fit of madness.
belies him] makes him speak falsely.

I bore my Annabella whilst she lived,
These hands have from her bosom ripped this heart.

Enter VASQUES.

Is 't true or no, sir?
Vasques.   'Tis most strangely true.   60
Florio. Cursèd man!—have I lived to—   *Dies.*
Cardinal.   Hold up Florio!—
    Monster of children, see what thou hast done,
    Broke thy old father's heart!—Is none of you
    Dares venture on him?
Giovanni.   Let 'em. O, my father,
    How well his death becomes him in his griefs!   65
    Why, this was done with courage. Now survives
    None of our house but I, gilt in the blood
    Of a fair sister and a hapless father.
Soranzo. Inhuman scorn of men, hast thou a thought
    T' outlive thy murders?
Giovanni.   Yes, I tell thee, yes;   70
    For in my fists I bear the twists of life.
    Soranzo, see this heart which was thy wife's;
    Thus I exchange it royally for thine,   [*Stabs him.*]
    And thus, and thus. Now brave revenge is mine.
                                        [*Soranzo falls.*]
Vasques. I cannot hold any longer. You, sir, are you grown   75
    insolent in your butcheries? Have at you!   *Fight.*
Giovanni. Come, I am armed to meet thee.
Vasques. No, will it not be yet? If this will not, another shall.—
    Not yet? I shall fit you anon.—Vengeance!

Enter Banditti.

Giovanni. Welcome! Come more of you, whate'er you be,   80
    I dare your worst.—   [*They surround and wound him.*]

_____

    67. *gilt in*] decorated with (perhaps with a play on 'guilt').
    71. *twists of life*] In classical mythology, lives were represented as threads
spun and cut off by the three Fates or Parcae.
    78. *will . . . yet?*] haven't I killed you yet?
    79. *fit you*] 'fix you up'.
    anon] soon.
    Vengeance] the 'watchword' (mentioned at V.iv.14) to summon the
Banditti.

O, I can stand no longer. Feeble arms,
Have you so soon lost strength?   [*Falls.*]

Vasques. Now you are welcome, sir! Away, my masters, all is
done; shift for yourselves, your reward is your own; shift   85
for yourselves.

Banditti. Away, away!   *Exeunt* Banditti.

Vasques. How d'ee, my lord? See you this? How is 't?

Soranzo. Dead; but in death well pleased, that I have lived
To see my wrongs revenged on that black devil.   90
O Vasques, to thy bosom let me give
My last of breath; let not that lecher live—O!   *Dies.*

Vasques. The reward of peace and rest be with him, my ever
dearest lord and master.

Giovanni. Whose hand gave me this wound?   95

Vasques. Mine, sir, I was your first man; have you enough?

Giovanni. I thank thee; thou hast done for me
But what I would have else done on myself.
Art sure thy lord is dead?

Vasques.   O impudent slave,
As sure as I am sure to see thee die.   100

Cardinal. Think on thy life and end, and call for mercy.

Giovanni. Mercy? Why, I have found it in this justice.

Cardinal. Strive yet to cry to heaven.

Giovanni.   O, I bleed fast.
Death, thou art a guest long looked-for; I embrace
Thee and thy wounds. O, my last minute comes.   105
Where'er I go, let me enjoy this grace,
Freely to view my Annabella's face.   *Dies.*

Donado. Strange miracle of justice!

Cardinal. Raise up the city; we shall be murdered all!

Vasques. You need not fear, you shall not. This strange task   110
being ended, I have paid the duty to the son which I have
vowed to the father.

Cardinal. Speak, wretched villain, what incarnate fiend
Hath led thee on to this?

Vasques. Honesty, and pity of my master's wrongs. For know,   115
my lord, I am by birth a Spaniard, brought forth my

---

116. *a Spaniard*] Spaniards were known for their skill in hiding malice
under a pretence of friendship.

country in my youth by Lord Soranzo's father; whom
whilst he lived I served faithfully; since whose death I
have been to this man as I was to him. What I have done
was duty, and I repent nothing but that the loss of my life   120
had not ransomed his.

Cardinal. Say, fellow, know'st thou any yet unnamed
Of counsel in this incest?

Vasques. Yes, an old woman, sometimes guardian to this
murdered lady.   125

Cardinal. And what's become of her?

Vasques. Within this room she is; whose eyes after her confession I caused to be put out, but kept alive, to confirm
what from Giovanni's own mouth you have heard. Now,
my lord, what I have done you may judge of, and let your   130
own wisdom be a judge in your own reason.

Cardinal. Peace! First, this woman, chief in these effects,
My sentence is that forthwith she be ta'en
Out of the city, for example's sake,
There to be burnt to ashes.

Donado.   'Tis most just.   135

Cardinal. Be it your charge, Donado, see it done.

Donado. I shall.

Vasques. What for me? If death, 'tis welcome. I have been
honest to the son as I was to the father.

Cardinal. Fellow, for thee: since what thou didst was done   140
Not for thyself, being no Italian,
We banish thee for ever, to depart
Within three days; in this we do dispense
With grounds of reason, not of thine offence.

Vasques. 'Tis well. This conquest is mine, and I rejoice that a   145
Spaniard outwent an Italian in revenge.   *Exit.*

Cardinal. Take up these slaughtered bodies, see them buried;

---

123. *Of counsel in*] in on the secret of.

124. *sometimes*] formerly.

131. *in your own reason*] of your own justice.

132. *this woman*] almost certainly Putana, but just possibly the dead body
of Annabella.

chief in these effects] who played a leading part in these doings.

143-4. *we do . . . offence*] 'we remit the full penalty in consideration of the
circumstances, without condoning your offence.'

And all the gold and jewels, or whatsoever,
Confiscate by the canons of the Church,
We seize upon to the Pope's proper use.   150
Richardetto. [*Discovering himself*] Your grace's pardon: thus long
    I lived disguised
To see the effect of pride and lust at once
Brought both to shameful ends.
Cardinal. What, Richardetto, whom we thought for dead?
Donado. Sir, was it you—
Richardetto.   Your friend.   155
Cardinal.   We shall have time
To talk at large of all; but never yet
Incest and murder have so strangely met.
Of one so young, so rich in Nature's store,
Who could not say, '*Tis pity she's a whore?*

                                            Exeunt.

                    FINIS.

    The general commendation deserved by the actors in their
presentment of this tragedy may easily excuse such few faults
as are escaped in the printing; a common charity may allow
him the ability of spelling, whom a secure confidence assures   5
that he cannot ignorantly err in the application of sense.

---

149. *Confiscate*] confiscated; stressed on the second syllable.
canons] rules.
150. *proper*] personal.
156. *at large*] fully.
158. *Nature's store*] the gifts of nature.

[Apology for Misprints]
    This postscript was probably added by Ford after most of the play had
been printed.
    3–5. *a common . . . sense*] 'it needs no great charity to assume that one who
uses words rightly also knows how to spell them.'